Tune Up, Drop In
or
Light Upon The Path

By: Peter F. Walker

This is a story of a musical journey, through a life of musical exploration and growth, resulting in a unique form of musical enlightenment. Over a life time the secrets of the guitar have been teased from both antiquity, and cutting edge modern fusion as the author has traced the musical footsteps of the world of guitar, to its roots, thousands of years ago, in the Veena of India and the worlds original "classical music" up to the guitar of the present day. It has been a long journey, and I am still on the path. I wish to share with the reader, how far I have come, how I got here, and where I am going.

Music is a unique language. It crosses all national and cultural barriers, and communicates perfectly. Not in specific words, but in feelings, and emotions, which are often best expressed only in this magical rubric. I hope to present here some light on the path for those who would follow, or for those who are interested in this fascinating instrument with its rich history, and amazing capabilities.

Ark Press
PO Box 584
Woodstock, NY
12498
ISBN: 978-1-939374-03-5

E-Mail Acousticman1@hotmail.com
Facebook: Peter Walker

Introduction - Baby Steps

Growing up in a musical family was a real "head-start" in many ways. Boston is a city full of colleges and universities and has high standards of education. That's especially true in the traditions of classical musical instruction. My father was from a generation that valued the classics in literature and music. Dad worked as a Hotel Manager but his primary occupation was photographer. He could play guitar and mandolin quite well. His other passion was Shakespeare.

I decided when I was about two years old that I wanted to play guitar, but the instrument was much to big for me. Try as I might, I could only play it lying flat on the floor, and quickly broke the strings trying to learn how to tune it. The mandolin was a different story. For learning the principles of fretting it was the perfect size fretboard for baby hands and fingers.

My mother was classically trained. In Boston in 1940 that meant she had graduated from the New England Conservatory of Music. She "majored" in Piano, and "doubled" in Clarinet and Tenor Saxophone. After her "recital" as a Pianist, Mom was a part of the first "all-women" orchestra in the US. Conducted by a grand Dame of Boston society it was quite the cutting edge event of it's time. She went from there to a brief career in a traveling wind ensemble, that played the luxury resorts of Maine and New Hampshire. It was there the my Dad found her and took her for Canoe rides with his mandolin, and spent evenings by the fire with her and his guitar. They married in 1932, during the great depression.

Before I was born and for the first ten years of my life Mom continued to study with her Professor from the Conservatory. We Lived in Medford, a suburb north of Boston in a large second floor apartment, on a shady side street. The grammar school was across the street. With trees to climb in the yard scaling the fence and using the school grounds for recreation became a routine from age 6 on. The two best features of the environment were the room in the front of the house, isolated and off the living room, which held the upright Steinway, and a huge library of piano music. Mom was serious about teaching us music, and bought one of those boards with staff music lines and removable notes, so that both my brother and I could read and write basic musical lines by the time we were four. The second feature was several blocks away in the form of "Pony boy stables"

For a suburban Boston kid having access to pony's and horses was a perfect counterbalance to the musical agenda being driven by my Mom. I think that she decided that since my father was molding my brother into becoming a scientist, (he did), that her agenda was to make me into a performing musician. Once a week, throughout my entire childhood, she would write a note to my teacher to have me excused from school on one pretext or another. We then went to a matinee performance of every vaudeville show that came through Boston for several years.

It was a stable life for the first ten years. Dad was working as the manager of the Beacon Chambers Hotel next door to the Massachusetts State Capital building and was gone long hours with his cronies and ubiquitous camera. Mom was a housewife, who spent a couple days a week playing with her professor and mentor from the New England Conservatory Louise Wright., As young as 4 years old I was enlisted to be the "page turner" as they thundered through hours of four handed Mozart. I was constantly reminded that real musical training required dedication and a rigorous practice regime. Eight hours a day divided as follows:

Two hours; scales, arpeggios, and hand or lip training exercises.

Two hours; exercise pieces, hand eye coordination, technique training.

Two hours; new repertoire, study and practice

Two hours; current repertoire, practice and polish.

Total 8 hours a day for each instrument chosen.

Too much for a young kid, who liked to play sandlot baseball, and avoided practice whenever possible. Both Mom and her professor friend would throw up their hands, but each school year they would start over again and make me start from the beginning and relearn again, what I had forgotten during a summer of swimming and fun. I think this repetition of the basics, and the idea of returning to the beginning is a good thing. When in doubt or at a plateau, as an adult, I often like to go back to basics, and look for things I have missed or ideas to develop.

The only music I did willingly as a child was a little piano, lots of harmonica, and basic fretting on the Mandolin. Strings for the guitar, were often missing, but the Mandolin was well maintained, and usually in tune.

Every once in a while, as I grew older in a household primarily dominated by the Piano

Mom would reach under the bed and drag out the two instrument cases which held her Clarinet and Sax. She was very skilled on the clarinet, which was a much more popular instrument then, but she rocked on the Sax. I have to say, it was a little shocking, but cool. I tried the Clarinet about the time I was as tall as it was. But although I could get a basic scale out of it, and even played it in a 3rd grade talent show, I didn't really have a lip for it. I preferred the harmonica, and was fascinated by strings.

In 1944 the war ended and the world was changing fast. Crystal radios were popular with the kids of my generation. My dad dragged home hundreds of pounds of army surplus radio transmitters power supplies, amplifiers and headsets. I loved the headsets, .For 15 cents you could buy a crystal to make a radio. 500 turns of thin copper wire on a piece of broomstick, a nail, an antenna and ground connection and a set of headphones were all that were required to make a radio that would bring in clear signal, under the covers, late at night, of the two main stations that had great reception in the northeast US due to the effect of the signal bouncing of the ionosphere.

My primitive hookup brought WWVA in Wheeling West Virginia and a renegade Texas border station that blasted an illegally strong signal from just across the border in Mexico with the Broadcast antennas arranged in an array to broadcast deep into the American heartland. With a good antenna it came in loud and clear in the army surplus earphones at 2:00 AM. Staying up that late was forbidden but it was easy to secrete the components and assemble them in a matter of moments under the covers. Long after my parents were asleep, I would tickle the crystal with a fine wire with the coil connected on one end to the radiator, and the other to the antenna wire hanging outside the bedroom window. The Grand Old Opry was on late, but very late was the Tex/Mex of the Mexican station with gospel, country, and on weekends rhythm and blues, with lyrics that were illegal in the USA. Exciting stuff for Boston in 1945.

The harmonica was my real instrument of choice during those years. With the strings on my dads guitar usually broken and the mandolin tremolo plectrum style difficult, I gravitated toward the portable, lyrical harmonica which had the added built in bass accompaniment. Playing "forwards" harp IE: playing in the key that the harp is manufactured in as opposed to "backwards harp" which plays in the dominant chord key of the harps designated original key. Playing for holidays, social occasions, pop songs, traditional folk material, reels, and even jigs. It was a popular instrument, and made a great traveling companion.

Later, as a teenager it was remarkably effective in diffusing dangerous situations, and distracting malefactors. Hitchhiking across the US in the early 50's was definitely dangerous. Survival skills for a 14 year old included mimicking local accents and passing under the radar of police, violent drunks, perverts, and general nosy troublemakers. For example, there was nothing more effective in a Mississippi roadhouse, when surrounded by suspicious and hostile rednecks straight out of deliverance, then a rousing chorus of "Dixie" which brought everyone to attention, followed by a couple choruses of "Yaller Rose of Texas" as I sashayed out the door and into the night. I could hear the voices behind my saying, "leave that boy alone, you fool, he done be playing "Dixie'. That a good old boy." This actually happened several times. Who says music isn't Magic.

It was thus no surprise to me at any rate that when I got into trouble at school, and took off, at fourteen, that I made a beeline first for the Grand Old Opry. I don't know if I had had vague dreams about playing there or if I just wanted to see the place I had been listening to for so many years. I was much too young then and didn't know anyone there. I went to one of the shows, stayed over a night in Nashville and continued on through the then still segregated deep south. It was a hairy hitch through Alabama, Mississippi, and on to Texas and the west coast. I figured out once that my average speed was about 25 miles an hour. It took 27 days to reach the west coast from Boston along the southern route. I returned East by the northern route through blizzards, Rocky Mountains, and the great plains. In between rides, walking along the side of the highways was a great chance to play as loud as I like and bend notes to my hearts content. I recently found a playbill from 1952 which announces that Peter Walker will be playing "Birth of the Blues" In the Dorchester High School Talent Show. Ten years later, in 1962, I would get a chance to play harp with all the old hands from the Opry, at one of the Newport folk festivals. I had forgotten all about until I came across a photo amongst Karen Dalton's papers. It is a wonderful thing when dreams come true. Even better when someone catches the moment with a camera.

At the end of my truncated high school adventures, I received an odd form of recognition from an unusual source. The entire Greater Boston Public School System had universal compulsory military training. This dated back to the civil war and was still very active during my era. Drill teams, marching formations, manual of arms, and close order drill were taught at least once a week at Dorchester high School by "Major McClusky" a colorful WW 2 vet who was immensely popular because he would open the side door to the gym during drill class and allow those who had em to smoke em. If the principal ever saw the blue cloud rising from the schoolyard by the gym door he never took official notice. The recognition came from Major McClusky just before graduation. The Annual "Schoolboy Parade" was an old Boston tradition and involved more than 20,000 students who marched as school units divided into 5 brigades of four thousand students each. It was pretty impressive. On the morning of the parade the Major promoted me in what he termed a "field commission" to Brigadier General. I was to be “Brigade Commander”. In command of my High school and two or three others. I would be Leading them in the parade, with my flag bearer walking three paces behind and two to the left wherever I went for the day. The flag bore my single silver star, as did I. There is a corollary to this anecdote which I think bears some relevance to my approach to my life and often to my music.

As the parade progressed on a hot June day, We came up between the Boston Gardens and the Boston Common. The plan was to turn and pass in review in front of the state house. There was a line of Senior Student Officers, all jocks, 12 abreast marching behind me. They kept calling to me, “now Walker, don't f*** this up. When we get to the corner, turn left. That’s LEFT. If you screw this up we are going to beat the s*** out of you.” The entire line of staff officers, Majors, Lt Colonels, and bird Colonels, tough kids from a tough school, took up the chorus, “yeah Walker, you better go left or else. They continued for the last hundred yards, threatening various forms of bodily harm and dire consequences if I failed to call the turn correctly to the LEFT. Out in front, I could see the flag bearer in my peripheral vision. . A couple steps before the center of the intersection I called out, “Coluuuuumn Right!” and as my foot hit the center “March!” I saw my flag dip and turn and the column turned in perfect order into the waiting crowds, flashbulbs, and reviewing stand. As I passed in front of the dignitaries, I was pulled out of ranks and brought up to the reviewing stand to “review my troops”.

I asked the major later why he had chosen me. He said “two reasons, in the history of the school several kids had run away to Florida, and a couple had run to California, but you were the first one to do both and in the same year. Second, you were the only SOB to show up this morning with a properly pegged (taken in) shirt.”

The moral of this story, was that if fate gives you the opportunity, you have to do what you know is right and not what anyone or everyone tells you to do. In life or sometimes, music.

This is a book about the guitar and not the harmonica. In 1952, age fourteen, upon my return to Boston after the solo journey to Florida and the California hitchhiking adventure. I made a deal with my then divorced mother and new step father to eschew further attempts to “run away” in return for my emancipation.

I continued in school, got a part time job, and bought a cheap guitar. It was then, in Dorchester, a suburb on the south side of Boston, that I began my real journey with this marvelous instrument.

LEVEL ONE
(amateur -obsessed – chord competent – hungry for more.)

Sore fingers, black diamond steel strings, high action cheap F hole guitars. It wasn't an easy beginning. What helped was the fact that sheet music was popular in the 50's. The local department store or music store had the top hits available with melody lines, piano arrangements, lyrics, and chord charts for ukelele and guitar for 75 cents each. It was cool to be able to play the top ten.

For a northeast city Boston had a surprisingly large country music base. In the 50's there were downtown clubs that were mirror images of the Texas roadhouses, well, maybe a little less violent. Well maybe a lot less but still quite violent. A couple radio stations blasted the country top ten, and in fact there were two "top tens" in Boston at the time, Country and Pop. Learning both slightly increased the cost of sheet music, but was a key to instant popularity. A friend of my mothers contributed a slightly better guitar, actually a couple damaged low quality broken instruments but I was able to get one set up fairly well. By the time I was ready to leave for college, I could play basic chords and accompany people singing.

Besides growing up watching my father read and play mandolin music, I found new information on guitar technique hard to find. The sheet music helped, for it usually included chord formations in pictographs, The only instruction books commercially available were nearly all manuals for "the plectrum style Spanish guitar' There was also a little information available from Carl Fisher Music on classical guitar, but besides the usual intro showing scales, the notation system offered almost no information which string or fret the written staff notation note was to be played on, and left the musician with multiple options. You had to figure the fingerings out by trial and error.

The local music stores that offered instruction only taught the plectrum style, and assumed every one wanted to play like the current electric players. I was interested in the acoustic capabilities of the instrument, but was left on my own to encounter other players who could contribute bits and pieces. Church sing-a-longs were popular in the fifties during my senior year in high school so I attended a lot of these. Over time I accumulated a basic repertoire of Gospel, Folk, current Country and Western, Pop, and a couple fragments of Classical music. I left for the University of Cincinnati with a basic six string guitar, some experience with two years of high school talent show productions, and a working knowledge of the basic chords for several keys. Also some song-leading skills.

UC (University of Cincinnati) had a student population of 10,000. There were two guitar players. Me, and one other young man whom I heard about but never met.

Almost immediately I became the accompanist for the schools drinking song sessions. At the school pub, as the young gentleman sang into the night of " Cheer Cincinnati" and "The Tables Down at Murray's in the Place where Louie dwells, etc etc ,". I did many many hours of strumming. I spent more time behind the guitar then in the study halls, and like a lot of students, more time hungry then not.

Cincinnati was across the river from Newport and Covington Kentucky, just a few miles away from the UC campus. Covington was great. It had girls, gambling, dancing and live music, for 1950's low prices. Country music and blues were really popular. I hooked up with a guy from the same rooming house, and aside from strumming for drunks, became for the first time a performer in that I accompanied my buddy Chuck who had lungs of steel and would belt out one blues after the other.

We invested in cowboy boots and wide brimmed hats, and called ourselves "Peter Potter and Chuckling Chuck". We did country music numbers and vaudeville humor. Working the bars for tips it was a great way to starve. We got a lot of blues requests, so we bought a book of blues lyrics with the sheet music arrangements, but they quickly all sounded the same, and our humor was pretty pale and stale. Mostly over-broad renditions of stock country routines and low grade vaudeville material..

At some point during this period I made several trips to La Grange, a suburb of Chicago, to visit a girl I was dating. She took me downtown on the 'The El" (elevated train) and showed me where the big music stores were. I would go there and drool over the instruments. Finally, hanging around in the Chicago music stores, I met other players, who staggered me with their skills. Blistering breakneck super accurate flat-picking for one. Mastery of the upper fretboard, scales at blinding speed, for another, I saw many examples of technical fluency. One became humble and respectful, with the sure and certain knowledge of how far I had to go.

The good news was that although the relationship with the college sweetheart didn't work out the guitar was now my new best friend and constant companion.

After a couple years in Cincinnati and 6 months in the Army reserve, I saved a few dollars, bought an old Chevy and returned to Boston, broke but with two years pre-law, more or less under my belt, and combined with the musical and independent traveling experience I was fairly worldly. I quickly got a job selling time on radio station WILD in Boston and began producing radio commercials on "spec" for various clients. The kind where two people would talk of the virtues of the clients business, with musical intros etc., humorous if possible. It was my first time editing tape, and doing over-tracks. Cutting and splicing tape, inserting leaders, these were the basic skills of becoming "a recording artist". I had no idea then how useful these skills would become.

The station was very promotion oriented, and was famous at the time for publicity stunts. The best one was a three day spree of announcements of the coming song to be played, and no matter what the announcer said, or how elaborate the introduction, the actual music was Peggy Lee's "Fever". They played nothing but "Fever" twenty four hours a day for three days. The interesting thing was that on the second and third days nearly the whole city tuned in to see if the station was still doing it. The station had gone from the least known in the city to being one of the most popular in just a few days. Peggy Lee wrote a great thank you letter to the station manager Peter Theg who framed it and put it over his desk next to the sign that said "the eagle is screaming". I moved up a notch in the station's staff, and became a roving news reporter, calling in on payphones from the scene of fire's and police activity with live on air reports using the name "Pete Winters" of the WILD mobile news patrol. I got to use the News Wagon as my personal ride. I loved it. The name stuck.

I rented a studio in the "St Botolph Studios" a landmark Boston building. In a classic artist studio with huge north facing windows and a parquet floor laid by Isabella Stewart Gardner for her friend and lover Whistler. It was a classic, and a great place to practice guitar and study. Downstairs in one studio lived a pair of piano teachers with back to back Stienways who taught show tunes, and poured drinks. Much more interesting was Palmer French a former genuine Full Professor of Music Theory. When I heard about his incredible credentials, I asked him one day if he would teach me theory. Just general music theory. He said yes and bent his nearly seven foot frame over the upright piano in his studio and began to explain the rubric of what music was. . I spent the next few months taking lessons at 5 dollars an hour about the story of Pythagorean theory and what happens mathematically when you pluck a string. He taught me the math behind what sounds harmonious and why. What a triad is and why it sounds pleasing to the ear. One of the more interesting things that he stressed is that harmony to some extent is subjective, and that in the 12 century Pope Gregory declared that all music must be played in perfect octaves, and all else is heresy, resulting in the Gregorian Chants, and that you could be burned at the stake for playing a Triad Chord or melody with odd intervals or thirds, or fifths, or horror of horror's 7ths let alone 9ths etc.

MECHAMANIA

It was about this time that my brother introduced me to a friend of his from MIT who was quite a character. Besides being an exotic MIT professor Jean Gilland was a great artist and played guitar very well. He began to show me my first Flamenco riffs, and greatly upgraded my chord and transition skills. We all knew that Jean's professorial credentials were bogus He had hacked into the MIT computer which was totally unsecured in those days, and assigned himself a degree, a salary, a laboratory, expenses, a phone line, and a pass to the faculty dining room. When questioned he would greatly thicken his accent and talk in Physics double speak in an odd French dialect. The listening party would always nod sagely as though they understood such esoteric principles. Jeans bullshitting skills were exceeded by his artistic skills, and his incredible repertoire of bawdy French and American folk songs was amazing.

For a few months we all spoke French, learned various bawdy ballads, and joined Jean in his passionate interest in race cars. We had vague ideas of forming a racing team using the Triumph and Sprite sports cars. This led to late night intensive discussions of gearboxes, drilled and lightened flywheels, removal of synchros, piston bores and double clutching over a brief period of "mechamania" resulting somehow in an exodus from Boston to California retracing my southern route of 6 years before. So, staggering our departure times over a couple months, traveling independently, my brother, Jean and I headed out west for the second time, to San Francisco. It was 1958. I was twenty years old.

Before leaving Boston we had generated some travel money by producing a quick publishing venture that printed programs for one of the smaller theaters. Robert J. Lurtsema, who was "Bostons voice of classical music" was a friend and was appearing in a production of "Streetcar Named Desire" in a "Back Bay: theater. I offered to produce the program at no cost to the theater. They agreed. It was a piece of cake. I decided on a 12 page program modeled on the "Playbill" model of the major theaters. It was mostly Ad's, The actual program in the center, and a small fluff about each actor. The rest, including the front and back cover, and at least half of most of the pages were all ad's. Selling the ads turned out to be much easier then I expected, and after a morning calling around I had sold all the space to restaurants who wanted the after theater patronage. In those days Vespa motor scooters were popular. Cutting through Boston traffic on the Vespa I picked up the ad copy and checks in a day or two and we started the paste up for the photo offset printers, from there to the binders. Prof. Jean Gilland was indispensable as a commercial artist and the entire project from inception to printers took about five days.

The Play ran for a few weeks, but then the theater made huge demands. They realized we had made a tidy profit on the initial program production and were demanding at least half of the advertising space, including the back cover and various other concessions. I took the tidy profit (a few hundred dollars), bought a "Woody" station wagon for a hundred bucks, put the Motor Scooter in the back, and took off. California here we come, but this time I was driving and not hitchhiking. We meandered, occasionally overheating through the still segregated and hostile deep south along the "southern route" west.

Having the motor scooter in the back was prudent. When the Woody broke down in Dallas, I drew upon my previous experience and went looking for a "drive-away" for the rest of the journey. In the late fifties and even today there are dealers who ship cars inter city. One of the most common was the Texas to California run. Dallas Car dealers always needed drivers. Sure enough there was a dealer who wanted a nearly new Cadillac with exquisite embroidered upholstery driven from Dallas to Sacramento. But there was one hitch, they needed a reference. "No problem" I said "just call Professor Gilland at MIT (Jean hadn't left yet) and he will vouch for me".

They called, and sure enough the switchboard put them through to Professor Gilland's Laboratory, and Jean shoveled the shit as only a pro can. In his thick French accent he inquired what kind of machinery Monsieur Walker would be driving, "a Maserati, perhaps, un Aston – Martin. perhaps"?? He assured the Dallas dealer that I was well known on the European racing circuit as a marvelous driver and totally responsible human being. He affected surprise and disappointment when he found out that I would only be driving a mere Cadillac and that from point to point rather than in a race. The Dallas car dealer was appropriately impressed by this ringing endorsement from a full professor at MIT. and gave us the car, and four days to deliver it. They also bought the broken down Woody for 75 dollars.

The following few days were a little like a scene out of Hunter Thompson's "Fear and Loathing in Las Vegas" only it took place in that Cadillac as we roared through Texas, Arizona, New Mexico and California. With the Motor scooter hanging out of the trunk, driving at times close to a hundred miles an hour, we ate our meals as we went, putting more wear and tear on that vehicle then one would have thought possible in just a few days. Arriving in SF, with two days to spare we drove around looking for a place to settle in. When I dropped the Cadillac off in Sacramento two days later It was late at night. The receiving dealer was closed, so I just left the keys and left for SF on the Motor Scooter. I am sorry to admit the Caddy was pretty well trashed. Kerouac would have been proud.

My brother followed a couple weeks later and made an attempt at a cross country speed record. Not officially, but he was determined it was going to be a real effort. In 1958 there was no Interstate Highway Infrastructure like we have today. The AAA was popular because of the incredible abuses and speed traps that had made cross country driving truly perilous for the unwary motorist. Some sections of roads were notorious. For a few dollars you could join AAA and they would provide four essential things.

1. Road Maps laid out for your journey in strips that could could be easily read while driving, containing specific local detail.

2. Warnings: notated in bright red on the maps were areas where they had received complaints of speed traps or police abuses.

3. Towing services and roadside repairs, up to 25$ no limit as to number of uses.

4. This was best of all; a "get out of jail free card". The membership card itself was good for up to 500 dollars in bail. If you timed it right and weren't opposed to gaming the system you could apply for your membership at the AAA office a week before you left for your trip and in addition to the permanent card that was received within a week and was good for bail you would also have the "temporary card"" also good for bail which was good for 60 or 90 days. So for your trip you had two "get out of jail free" cards It was like monopoly.

My brother was driving a Jaguar XK140 MC Convertible Roadster. The Jag had incredible acceleration and cornering characteristics. He fitted the strip maps into a holder where he could instantly see the terrain and distance to the state lines, and took off. 1st gear was good to 40 miles and hour 2nd was good up to 80, third to 120 and 4th was good up to 140 miles an hour with terrific torque. Every Saturday he would tune it up and raced every car in Boston up Belmont Hill. It was a fast car, but more significant was its stability in a curve. He outran the police a dozen times. He became accustomed to seeing flashing red lights disappear behind him. On one occasion he noticed that the state line was only thirty miles away and was through curving mountainous terrain. He floored it and got away. Twice he was caught in the deep south but the AAA cards let him keep right on going. Finally he was caught in Texas and paid a healthy fine, but still he made it from Boston to SF in under four days, which was considered amazing at the time. He went to work as a bartender in the Bagel shop and became a fixture on the North Beach Scene for a while. Jean Gilland arrived a few week later, but SF was his hometown and he was occupied with his true love who had arrived from France. .

BEATNIKS

By random chance or destiny I wound up renting a tiny apartment one block from the Bagel Shop in North Beach for about thirty bucks a month. It was the height of the "beatnik" era. I hung around in the Coffee Gallery, and Bagel shop with Ron Rice, Eric Nord and Bob Kaufman, and played my guitar. With the income from a job working for the SF city directory, I bought a much better guitar, and a used but beautiful Jaguar XK120 Roadster. Over in the Sausalito houseboats on weekends, we camped in the wheelhouse of one of the huge old ferryboats. John McFeeley was a north beach politico and was the "jazz candidate" for congress from the district that included North Beach. He lent out his 26 foot sailboat to anyone who asked, so it was a busy fun time. In Sausalito I met my first contemporary folksingers, and playing with them became the weekend norm.

One day in the Bagel shop I was approached by a young black singer named Jon Bonet, who asked me to accompany him singing. I said sure, and wound up playing several gigs with him at "The Purple Onion" and "Hungry Eye". Those were my first real gigs.

One of my Bagel shop cronies was Jim Gurley. The same Jim Gurley who would play with Janis Joplin ten years later in "Big brother and The Holding Company"
His girl friend Nancy, bought him a 15 dollar guitar, and it was my privilege to show him his first chords. He became a world class guitarist in just a couple years, practicing day and night. It was, for him, a magnificent obsession. For the next few years we remained close friends and would hang out once a year for a week or so in Detroit. His rapid progress always amazed me.

Lord Buckley was popular in North Beach, and did regular gigs at the Coffee Gallery. I got to meet him and he dubbed me "Prince Peter". His renditions of "The Nazz" and "Jonah and the Whale" were inspiring and his general viewpoint was infectious. If Richard Lord Buckley was a preacher, I was a convert. I wanted to be a performer, but was painfully aware that I still lacked many skills. I was still an amateur, and not sure where to go from there. I was content for the moment to be able to play for others, and probably could have worked with a group playing 2'nd guitar, and occasionally did, but I was eager to learn more. After a year or so, Working in Sf and Monterrey, I packed up the Jag and returned to Boston. The coffee house and Folk

Music scene were just getting off the ground.

The "Golden Vanity" was a Boston Coffee House run by Carl Bowers. To give you an example of the economic scale of things, one regular performer who packed the house was Joan Baez who quit when Carl refused to pay her more than twenty five dollars a performance. Within a year Joan was making five thousand dollars per appearance. and the Golden Vanity was history. But not before a year of wonderful shows. Carl liked blues, and contemporary songwriter/balladeers. It was a great education. As a habitue I got to meet and hang our with every name in the blues and folk world that was still touring at the time.
Sonny Terry and Brownie McGhee were regulars, appearing every few weeks. The performers slept upstairs, and were paid 250 a week. One night there were two ladies of the night that were well known in Boston at the time as Joanie and Jeanie "The Gold Dust Twins". For their own reasons they decided it would be cool to spend the night with Sonny. That sweet old blind harmonica player had one of the best nights of his life. Because I had performed the introduction he assumed that I was somehow responsible. I last saw Sonny about a year before he died in 86, he was still thanking me for Joanie and Jeanie. I loved Sonny. When an opportunity came along in the early seventies to do a harmonica book for "Oak Publications" I gave the contract to Sonny. He told me later that he made very good money from it. I was very happy for him. In a way he was a both a hero and a peer. What he expressed with his instrument was pure raw emotion.

The Golden Vanity hosted Lightning Hopkins, Blind Lemon, John Lee Hooker, Josh White, Judy Collins, Tom Rush, Jackie Washington, Rolf Caen, Mississippi John Hurt, Sonny Terry and Brownie Mcghee, among many others. As a special favor to me Carl booked NYC flamenco guitarist Steve Kahn. Steve had studied in Spain in Jerez de la Frontera and is a terrific and dedicated player. It was my first time up close watching a good flamenco player work. It was a scene unto itself. The Boston student population loved it. I tried once or twice do do a number in an odd open mike moment but it was still painfully obvious to me that I still had a long way to go. I think that It was fair to say that I had reached Level One. IE: amateur -obsessed – chord competent – hungry for more.

I got a job at The South End Music Center as a guitar teacher and began to teach underprivileged kids to play basic chords and scales. Paid two dollars an hour but for the first time in life I was truly happy and doing what I wanted to do. It wasn't performing or even learning but it was making my living from music however peripheral. And left me plenty of time free to explore further.

With apologies to those to whom all this is obvious.

Appendix 1: CHORDS: Palmer French string theory. basic 1st position chords. Especially C A G E D also Tonic dominant and sub dominant. Basic Phrygian progression.

Appendix 2: seven short Flamenco Pieces

Appendix 3: Indian Raga notations and examples

Appendix 4: SCALES: basic and slightly advanced basic seven, with special fingerings for hand development. Overall fretboard Pattern.

LEVEL TWO

"Magnificently obsessed, curious, driven, still not professionally competent, but growing like a weed."

It was great to be out of the world of radio sales, and endless commercials, and to live entirely in the world of Music. It was nirvana, it was priceless, it was peace. Teaching at the South End Music Center didn't pay much but it was good karma. Most of my students were underprivileged and some were handicapped. They all made steady progress in learning basic scales and chords, which was all I was really qualified to teach.

For a couple months I also worked at a music store in Wellesley, Mass. teaching basic guitar. I noticed that they sold a lot of instruments and accessories to the students, and it was the backbone of their business. I swiped a couple wholesale catalogs, and started looking for an opportunity. Over time some of my Boston students needed better instruments, so at some point I made a trip down to NYC and toured the various musical warehouses and wholesale suppliers. The discount music stores in midtown NY offered 40% of list price and the wholesalers offered 50% discount. I was able to offer my students good quality instruments at discount prices, and still make a couple bucks.

Shortly after that I was over in Boston's Beacon Hill Ritzy residential district, and visited a friend, Stanley Stansky, who had a book store that was failing. I offered to rent one wall of his store for a hundred dollars a month, which enabled him to meet his rent and stay in business.

I hung a few guitars, a banjo and some string sets on the wall. Also a little sign in the window that said "guitar lessons". Since I taught in the afternoon I had mornings free to roam the antique districts of the north end of Boston. After a while the shop owners would save stuff for me and it was these good relations with the professional antique hunters that made it possible to build a music business. The formula for buying antiques was and still is: Offer what it is worth to you. If that's enough great. If not, pass.

I paid Stan a commission on sales, and they took off. We sold out the wall in the first week. Even better, I quickly became fully booked with students at the princely sum of 5 dollars an hour. I rushed back to NYC for more guitars and enjoyed a respite from abject poverty and was caught up in creating a musical rubric. The doors of access to information were opening. Music sales were outselling books ten to one, so after a couple months I rented the rest of the space and fully stocked it. The front of the shop became a music store, and the rear became a repair shop. Stan had good carpentry skills and applied these to common sense guitar repairs. I brought tools, clamps, rosettes and books on instruments, and supplies from H.L. Wild on 9th street in NYC. He bought a couple books on guitar making and quickly became quite adept. So now there was a retail outlet and a repair shop. The reason for the instant success was the foot traffic. Passing by the small shop window was a greater part of the population of Beacon Hill. They were educated, affluent, and intellectually curious, they loved music. The tiny store thrived.

In the evenings I often hung around at "Tulla's Coffee Grinder" in Harvard Square. Tulla's was the first folk music coffee house in Cambridge, and was unique. The clientele were very much like the people of beacon Hill, but they were younger and their were a lot more of them.

I noticed a shop for rent on Mt Auburn Street, and made inquires. A month later The "New Scene Folklore Center" opened it's doors for business.

"If you want to learn to play you have to play with guitarists who are better then you." the "Cambridge Folklore Center" was an immediate gathering place for musicians to relate, swap, strut, huddle, jam, bitch, moan and play some more. The long wall of instruments included a great collection of playable stuff and there was no shortage of volunteers to do the playing.

Information poured in. It was great. Because I was a music store I could wholesale access music instruction books, odd instruments, everything available through the traditional music suppliers. There were middle Eastern importers in NYC also. Dumbecs bouzoukis, and cheap imported banjos dressed up the wall and provided interesting tools for experimentation. One of the best was the "devils fiddle" a "one man band sort of thing with percussion actuated by a bow, and a devils head and cymbal on top of a 5 foot stick. Playing all the folk instruments in sequence made a good show.

I did frequent radio shows, and occasional lecture demo's at some of the local schools. Like the robot in "#5 is alive" I devoured the INPUT. It came in all forms.

I had only been open in Harvard Square (Mt Auburn Street) for a couple months when I 8 – 10 year old kid came in one Saturday morning. He was carrying a baseball bat. The instruments were all displayed hanging from a wall and in a long line of guitar stands along the wall underneath the hanging instruments. I viewed him as potential trouble from perhaps accidentally knocking over one of the instruments. It was a kid, right? Kids do things like that. So I said "Hey Kid, watch out for the instruments." "Can I try one?" he asked. I was cautious but indulgent. "Sure, which one?" He pointed to a good steel string guitar " "how about that one" he said. I pulled out the stool, sat him down on it, checked him for zippers or buckles that might injure the instrument and carefully place it in his hands. "go ahead" I said with just a hint of a sarcastic sneer. He looked up, "Travis picking or carter style?" he said, referring to two basic folk styles of playing. "Travis" I said, and he proceeded to do a perfectly credible job of San Francisco Bay Blues a classic Travis piece. He shifted easily into a carter picking piece and finished up with a little flat picking display. Impressive.

He stood up and handed back the guitar and pointed to a banjo. "can I try that?" he said. "you play banjo too?" I was getting respectful. "Do you want to hear Scruggs style (as popularized by legendary bluegrass players Lester Flat and Earl Scruggs) or frailing" (Pete Seeger style) he said with total innocence. "Scruggs" I said, and off he went. Followed by frailing, and a couple other styles I had never seen before. It went on like that for more than an hour. He went right down the wall playing all the instruments in at least one style usually two or even three. He reached the mandolins and played both "Potato bug" (rounded back) and "flat back" in traditional and bluegrass styles. He finally reached the auto harp, and holding it in the upright position, he asked. "Traditional or Stoneham style?" (referring to Mike Seeger's style on Folkways recordings.). I was incredibly impressed and told him so, and told him he was welcome back anytime.

It turned out that his father was a Harvard Professor who came in for something a couple weeks later. "You know" I said to him "that you son is a genius". "why is that?" he asked. I told him "because he can play every instruments in the shop, and in every style"."Oh, that" he said, "last year it was baseball, he could name every player in both leagues and their batting averages." What a privilege it was to be a member of the marvelous Harvard community, with its high standards of excellence and "permission" to excel.

The Folklore Center

After about 6 months a larger store became available in the same block and I moved to the larger quarters. Stansky built some teaching rooms, in the back and I retained the Beacon Hill store as a second outlet and repair shop. Things were working out.

There was an antique dealer who prowled the flea markets of Vermont and New Hampshire with an old farm truck and would pass through every few months with lots of great old instruments. Vega "tuba phone" banjos, fret-less 5 strings, antiques, rare chord harps, Gibson, Washburn, and Martin guitars, and other early American instruments. Eventually this fellow brought me both of the instruments that I sold to Karen Dalton. Beautiful exquisitely balanced Gibson 6 and 12 strings. One day he brought me an old Ramirez with pegs from Madrid. 6 years later I would use this guitar to play "Rainy Day Raga" for Vanguard, but all that came later, after Spain, after Africa, after Mexico and Hollywood.

The folk music boom was booming and the demand was becoming difficult to supply. There were only two 12 string guitars available at the time. A "Stella" for 45 dollars, and a Vega for 250 dollars. Sensing a price vacuum in the mid-range, I went to NYC and bought a couple dozen guitar bodies from a wholesaler, and separately two dozen 12 string guitar necks from H. L. Wild on 9th street. Stansky set to work attaching the necks to the bodies, and setting up the actions. They sold for 185 dollars and sold out in a few weeks. I needed more guitars.

I went back to NYC and prowled around the warehouses and musical supply houses. At the same supplier who had sold me the guitar bodies I noticed a chicken wire room packed with broken guitars. "Whats those? I asked. "The Favilla factory went out of business" he said, "that's their left over unfinished or broken stock". Favilla was an excellent maker of both nylon "classical" and steel string guitars, who used really high quality materials, I bought the entire lot of over a hundred instruments for 65 dollars each. Stansky went to work repairing them and they provided a much needed infusion of high quality bargain priced stock. Still the demand was insatiable.

I decided to go to Mexico and buy guitars. It was a life changing decision.
Early in 1962 I enlisted the help of one of my cronies who was an instructor at the Matson Karate Academy in Boston, who had experience in Mexico, and spoke basic Spanish. We took a plane to Mexico City.

I ran into a professional guide and resident of Mexico D.F. (Mexico City) downstairs from the US Embassy at "Sanbornes de la Reforma" a very upscale restaurant and retail store chain. Senor "Don Alexander" was a singer in a large Mex City stage band. He was well dressed, educated, knew a great many important people in the city and knew how to find both all the guitar makers, both large and established and the one band saw garage size makers. He also knew all the best restaurants and the fabulous pulsing night life of the largest city in the western hemisphere. Talk about FUN!!!!

We toured the guitar factories by day, and enjoyed the rich exotic culture, food, Sanbornes. and the model infested super upscale cafe's of "Calle Hamburgoso" at night. I soon became comfortable walking around the city late at night, and made a life decision to learn the language. I loved the culture but couldn't communicate beyond the basics.

The guitars flowed north by the planeload and were generally of remarkably good quality. The cheapest ones twisted like pretzels after not many months in the New England climate but the slightly better ones and all of the high quality ones fared fine.

I settled on a standard model that sold for 15 dollars in Mexico D.F., arrived in Boston for about 25 dollars and sold wholesale for about 38 dollars and retailed for about 75. It was a very good business model. I worked with the local banks and learned how to do "cash projections" and short term business financing. Interesting and productive times.

Back in Cambridge the teaching was booming. I had a small but reliable staff of teachers that included among others Tim Hardin. He was a very good teacher. He would lock eyeballs with the student and say "do what I do". All his students played exactly like him.

Joan Baez, and most other visiting players and visitors bought strings and picks, and tried the very rare Martin "45" series guitars. Tim Hardin, Karen Dalton, Jose Feliciano, Sandy Bull, Hamza al Din, and hundreds of others all spent afternoons playing the different instruments and jamming. It was a scene.

Because it was a music store I had access to the Carcassi Method for classical guitar, and we maintained a large selection of OAK publications and "sing outs" for the Folk aficionados and sheet music for the classical buffs. Sor, Tarrega, Asturias, it was really basic stuff, but so far ahead of where I was a few years before. For the first time I discovered the system of notation called "tablature" with its 6 instead of 5 line staff which made it so much easier to read music written or notated for guitar.

When Folk musician/singer/songwriter Rolf Caen came back from a musical sabbatical in Spain the world took another turn. Rolf had been living among the gypsies. He had a fragile sonorous Domingo Esteso guitar with peg tuners from Madrid. It was one the rarest and best flamenco guitars from one of the best builders ever. He was selling taped lessons for each of the basic flamenco forms. Intensive and driven, he sold the tapes along with live lessons. I bought four tapes and took four lessons and learned my first genuine basic riffs. Like the junkie who gets his first access to "china white" I was hooked now for sure. I had reached "Level Two".

Magnificently obsessed, curious, driven, still not professionally competent, but growing like a weed. And now I knew where to go to learn more.

Appendix 3
Alegrias, Soleares, Farruca, Taranta, Simple versions with corrected tablature.

LEVEL THREE

The Kennedys, Spain, Tangier, Dallas, Mexico

I didn't realize it at the time but I had become a genuine “Folk Musician” my travels and studies had been a view of the segregated nation at the end of world war two viewed through a musical eye, and experienced first hand on the ground. I wasn't a “Folk Singer”, wasn't a “vocalist”, but I considered myself to be an “instrumentalist” and, besides the harmonica, played most instruments with strings, especially antique folk instruments.

I was, and always will be primarily absorbed with the Spanish guitar. It was a life decision made when I was a child. I had tried other instruments but despite having handled many banjo's and violins I was notably inept on both. I loved the auto-harps, dulcimers, double dulcimers, chord harps,ukelins, and other uniquely American hybrid instruments that were easily found in antique and thrift shops during the early 1960's. I was fascinated by the guitar. It was a link to my father. Like life and death, it was a mystery.

It was this interest in folk music and instruments that brought me into contact with Edward M. Kennedy during the JFK administration. It was 1962 and Edward M. had appeared during the plans for a 72 hour “Hootenanny” in Cambridge, Mass.

He was parked across the street in a car with Mass plate #2. I approached out of curiosity and we talked for a few hours about the goals and motivations for the event. At the end of the evening, he offered his support. The initial intended beneficiary of the planned three day concert was a Fund maintained by the Kennedy's for handicapped children. After discussions the beneficiary was changed to Children's Hospital in Boston Mass. To give the proceeds to the Kennedy fund might be seen as political, while Children's Hospital was a broad spectrum treatment center with no political ties.

The Event was conceived out of legal research into “marathons”, They were declared illegal in the late 20's and I was curious why. It turned out one of the reasons is because they attracted large crowds. So, performances in Massachusetts were limited to 72 hours. That put the kibosh on marathons, but it left open the possibility of a 72 hour three day event that was unheard of in 1962 because it hadn't been done since 1928.

I thought that with so much folk talent available I would try to do it and got a permit to stage it in my store window as the stage, block off the street, and mount the speakers in the vacant upper windows of the building at 91 Mt. Auburn Street. I was the sole instigator and guilty party. When Len Chandler arrived from NYC it became a movement event and really took off.

I have to give credit to the Harvard Community for "permission to excel", the encouragement of people like Tim Leary and others at Harvard and in the music community inspired me to reach out to be my best. I did this at a time when I was having success importing instruments from Mexico City. Regular trips to Mexico City had resulted on buying up the output of most of the larger guitar factories and shipping them airfreight to the loving arms of the Boston student population. Mexico City in 1962 was an incredible life style and the guitars were great, so was the music. Staging this event was a sort of celebration of success.

The Senator's appearance and encouragement occurred on the evening before the event, and was shortly after I had to actually physically throw someone out who was apparently an undercover agent trying to make trouble.

When I went to see who was watching in Mass plate #2 and asked who's plate it was. Edward M. said it was one of the governors but that he had borrowed it. He joked about borrowing state cars, I thought that was interesting. We talked, me sitting on a crate beside his car window, in the parking lot of Furman's Liquor Store facing the Cambridge Folklore center with the window dressed as a stage and lit, ready for the event to begin, The Event was on the front page of the Boston Broadside that week, press releases were out, it was in play for sure. The Holy Modal Rounders, Len Chandler, Tim Hardin, and hundreds of others lined up to play over the next three days. A couple of top DJ's volunteered as hosts. Stations set up live remotes.

Having the "blessing of the Kennedy's" was fantastic in terms of cooperation from the print and broadcast media in Boston. We were on the air with live remotes every 20 minutes on every major radio and TV station for the next three days and the interviews and crowds were constant. The main problem became crowd control. As the crowds grew over the next three days, a few police officers directing traffic became platoons of police maintaining a perimeter. Finally the entire fire department was out trying to "make a hole" in the huge crowds that were blocking the streets of Harvard Square and grid-locking the Harvard Commencement Exercises that were unfortunately scheduled for the third and peak evening of our "Hootenanny". The entire event was a huge success. The Cambridge Chief of Police said that I would "never do another event in his town again." I viewed this as a compliment.

Security had been provided by local Cambridge police officers hired by the platoon with sergeant and four or six patrolmen. MIT and Harvard had high tech high paid security forces, but the city of Cambridge had one of the lowest paid police forces in the country at the time. It was remarkably cheap per hour. We started with one then eventually three platoons of officers.

The Fire department was called out on the third night when the crowd ran over 35 thousand people clogging mount Auburn Street, Harvard Square. Most significantly access by car to the Harvard Commencement Ceremonies held in Harvard Stadium was blocked. The bridge over the Charles River was completely closed and the alumni and bigwigs were tied up in a classic gridlock The chief got a lot of flack but it was not an intended consequence. It definitely added to the general hubbub. The crowd remained under control, but just barely. For a first attempt at a major event it was a remarkable success. It was followed by tragedy.

I was in Union Square in NYC just leaving "Eastern Music", a wholesaler, when I heard over a passing car radio that JFK had been shot. I headed directly for the airport and the shuttle home and upon landing learned that he was gone. Things went to "Hell in a Hand-basket" really quickly. The "Folk Music movement stopped dead in bit's track and the demand immediately fell off for instruments.

I had met the girl of my dreams and had fallen in love. Her parents were violently apposed to our union. A friend of Tim Leary's and mine had been arrested at the border with a pound of pot. I had paid his bail and appealed to the Kennedy's for clemency for him. Now that the Kennedy's were out of power it was a whole new ball game. The Feds were convinced I was bringing in more then just guitars and were harassing my shipments. My crates were stuck at customs at the airport. None of it was true. Consumer? sure, supplier, NO.

The world was changing rapidly, with Kennedy out of the way, the political climate was changing drastically and dramatically. I wanted to go to Spain, study the guitar, and export instruments.

SPAIN, TANGIER

I closed the doors of the Folklore Center, packed a bag. took my Ramirez Guitar, stopped in New York to pick up the woman who was to become my most significant inspiration, my companion and best friend throughout the key moments of my musical discovery and development. She climbed out the window of her parents house with 3 suitcases and a make up case. I had brought a suitcase for her with her things from Boston, my own suitcase, and a guitar. We took the night Icelandic Flight to Luxemburg. Two days later after a 24 hour flight with a stopover in Iceland. we were having hot chocolate in bed in Paris. From there by train to Barcelona, and then south to Valencia . In Valencia we rented an enormous apartment fort 65 dollars a month, checked in with the Embassy for English teaching work, and found both an excellent guitar supplier and a Flamenco teacher. Mr. Pappas sold meat in the daytime and taught flamenco in the evenings. He taught me my Alegrias, Soleares, and Tarantas.

The plan had been to live in Valencia, study, and export guitars, but the funding never came through. Faced with dwindling resources, we made the decision to head for Tangier. The theory was that the incredible low cost of living would enable us to survive on a tiny budget. After an interminable ride on a third class train, we arrived at Algeciras and took the ferry to Morocco. The Arabic music throbbed from every cafe, shop and bazaar. I had been to Casablanca the year before and Algeria, so I was accustomed to the chaos and hubbub of the culture. We arrived in the "Socco Chico" (Little Square) of the "Casbah" of Tangier with seven pieces of luggage and seven dollars. It was the winter of 1963. It was to be a long and difficult winter.

I later called it "survival school". Over a winter's time through the cold and rainy season and Ramadan the music pulsed from everywhere only interuppted be the calls to prayers.

There was an expat colony living in the impossibly cheap Arab quarter. Their were a few other English speakers for some degree of mutual support and advise. The soul source of potential income was either selling possessions or one could compete with the locals for guide work. English speaking tourists from the tour boats that appeared in the harbor were more likely to trust other English speakers.

The music was worth the trip. The North African music was and is an important link with its exotic melodies and scales. it was one of the clues to eventually unraveling the

“Musical Mysteries of the Orient“ Although I got quite sick from the food and primitive conditions, it was worth the trip, both to learn about the culture and the music.

Eventually my brother sent airfare and a return to the US was possible, I reopened the Folklore center, but my heart really wasn’t in it and the folk movement was flaccid at best. I began to plan to drive to California in the fall of 64.

DALLAS

The following year (after the assassination of JFK) we scheduled the second "Marathon" event in Boston's Copley Square in support of SNCC and Dr. Martin Luther King. The Student Non-Violent Coordinating Committee was the cutting edge of Dr. Kings activities. Len Chandler had sold me on the idea of supporting Dr. King the previous year. It was a smaller event, Taj Majal showed up and filled in the blank hours with "Louie Louie". Taj is a genuine American Hero, like Bobby Neuwirth, Sandy Bull and many other unsung "keepers of the faith". The newspapers covered it. It had been originally scheduled for the Hatch Memorial Shell, but when the Metropolitan Transit Authorities found out the event was to be in support of Dr. King they pulled the plug. I accused them in the papers of being racist, and although it generated press for the cause, I will never do an event (ever they said) on Boston Park Property. OK so plan B was a church in Copley Square.

Through the rest of the summer I sold out the instrument stock, and closed the stores for good.

It was almost fall I was planning to drive across country, headed for California. I had spent the previous winter in Spain and North Africa and had my first direct experiences with the Gypsy and Arabic cultures and music. I wasn't a professional player yet but was an advanced student for sure.

At the request of the editor of the Cambridge Chronicle, who was a friend of the Kennedy family, I stopped in Dallas for a couple months. It was an unusual request but not really. I was only in my mid twenties but had a very unusual amount of experience as a traveler and observer.

I had first been to Dallas in 1952 during the second of two cross country trips as a runaway 14 year old hitchhiking and traveling with a harmonica playing Stephen Foster tunes and "Dixie" and "Yellow Rose of Texas". No one bothered me. It was a time when phone calls were still a nickel, and vagrant travelers were sent to chain gangs to break rocks for their dinner.

Dallas and South Texas was a dangerous and well armed place of which the family had absolutely no first hand knowledge from the ground.

At the time that the request was made, I had by then a respectable track record of survival and functionality in the streets of Paris, Gypsy Spain, Arab “Barrios and Medinas” in wartime Algeria and the “Casbahs” of Casablanca, and Tangier in Morocco. They knew knew I was comfortable walking around late at night in Mexico City, and had been to Dallas several times as early as 1952. They wanted the benefit of the viewpoint of someone with good analysis, and observance skills. They said that they were interested in my “perceptions”.

I went ahead with the trip. Leaving in the early fall my lady and I headed west, and stopped in Dallas for a while. I stayed in Dallas for a couple months, long enough to play in every venue within 20 miles of the city center, and to gather my “impressions” for the benefit of the family. Most “Private Clubs” and Restaurants, and honky-tonks, would allow me to play a set, and we were actually very well received. They did think that we looked a little strange, but that was to be expected after a winter in Tangier. I Made friends with other musicians who worked in the downtown clubs, and got a job playing Spanish Music on a weekly radio show broadcast direct from one of the clubs operated by one of Jack Ruby's peer group.

Living in a rented room near Oswald's place in the “Oak Cliffs” area of Dallas helped to impart a sense for what was probably real as apposed to conjecture in the life of this world class “Patsy” who was apparently manipulated and set up as a cover for the what we now know to be a triangulation of fire by professional marksman under the supervision of members of the intelligence community with the support of key figures in Federal law enforcement, organized crime, and a cabal of politicos who stood to benefit from both the continuing war, and the privatizing of the countries silver bullion reserves, as well as many other political and economic benefits. The process of uncovering all this is ongoing and will be for years to come.

The idea then was to gather fragments, that by themselves were not important but when put together with other facts helped to flesh out a more realistic picture of what had happened. The most significant scrap of “intel” I gathered was that: if all of Jack Ruby's peer group were into dealing drugs, arms, and woman, wasn't Jack? And assuming that was so what did that mean?

Oil money was so plentiful that apartments were a popular investment, driving the market down with fabulous amenities. Drapes, pools, free rent incentives. The rich were very rich, the poor, plentiful.

Living in an older rundown neighborhood of Oak Cliffs gave a sense of the poverty and desperation of the inhabitants, almost like a trip back in time to a different America. People who live under the close scrutiny of landlords who collect rent weekly, insurance policy agents who collect quarters and dimes for small burial policies at the door, cheap food in cheaper markets, I guess the point was that Oswald obviously struggled economically which would have made him vulnerable to manipulation. I'm not solving the crime here, just picking up stray scraps some of which like the Ruby info later turned out to be significant.

One Saturday night two federal agents who worked for Bobby Kennedy's justice department showed up at the club. They recognized me from Boston/Cambridge, and said hello. We had been introduced in 62 by a Cambridge Police sergeant who was always benevolent and helpful not only then but over the years afterward. They were quite surprised to see me and it showed.

Because they were dressed like young Justice agents they appeared to be what they were. Their greeting was noticed by the bouncer and chief henchman of "da boss" who's eyebrows shot up upon witnessing the exchange.

I was partially pleased to see these guys showing up to do background research on Ruby's peers and finding me already "imbedded" but concerned that I had been discovered to be more than just a traveling itinerant musician who played Spanish music. From the Dallas club owners perspective, the recognition by the clean cut well dressed young federal agents was a red flag.

It was two days later that I overheard a conversation between the Boss and his Number 1. I had just arrived and paused in the stairwell which led to the upstairs "Club". The odd acoustics of the building brought their conversation to me clearly from the back office. They were discussing their plans for me and my wonderful Lady for the coming weekend. (It was) not good plans. I crept back down the stairs, got into my car, stopped in the cliffs, silently made the emergency hand sign for LGTFOHN (lets get the **** out of here NOW) and less than 45 minutes later passed the Dallas city limits headed west, free and underground. We went on to play music in Monterrey, Cannery Row, Berkeley, North Beach, Marin.

Living "off the grid" continued to be interesting but without major incident until Puerto Vallarta in the Winter of 65.

PUERTO VALLARTA

In PV there was a thriving colony of movie people and psychedelic experimenters. Living underground had become a habit ever since Spain and Africa. There was a pleasant freedom to being anonymous.

One skill of living on the road or in a resort community like PV was to create the impression that you wanted in terms of a paper trail. For example: you could leave things in your bag or room to mislead someone searching through your stuff. You could control who the locals thought you were. It was useful.

Also from North Africa, We had fallen into the habit of using a private language of Arabic hand signs, very useful for communicating privately right in front of others. Native Americans do it all the time. They use the same hand signs throughout both continents. After spending a winter in Tangier with 7 dollars, deceptions and misdirection had become a basic, routine, instinctive recreational reaction.

At one point in LA, after an old Cadillac that we had bought in Malibu for 50 dollars broke down, for example, we walked onto a car lot and drove away in a car legally. They wanted the old Cadillac, it was a rare model, and they assumed (mistakenly as it turned out) that they would be able to repossess the few hundred dollar car we were buying if we didn't pay. You can't repossess a car with a vigilant loyal German Shepard in it. No money, no papers, no job, just gypsy hutzpah (and a reference from John who delivered an Oscar worthy performance, in the role of "Super Star worried about his poor personal assistant, batman, and transportation coordinator who was unfortunately without wheels at the moment. Hmmm and he was very interested in the Classic Bentley in the corner, but not just now, later, must run ta ta"). Underground is the norm if your living in the wind. We were definitely "blowing in the wind". A Gurgifian whirlwind. Identity's were disposable.

Like music practice it just became part of daily life.

The Movie Colony was thriving. PV was still an isolated paradise accessible only by air or a very bad dangerous road from the north. I had come in over the mountains from the

East, first gringo ever to come directly over the mountains from Guadalajara, in a Oldsmobile Hard top convertible held together with baling wire and prayers. It was an incredible adventure and the story appears on the album “Freedoms” as “fifty Miles” (on two flat tires). I still go back to visit the places on the road in the song. The truth was that the car didn't make it.

If you draw a straight line from Guadalajara to Puerto Vallarta at the high point halfway over the mountains is the Shangra-la like town of Marscota. The terrain is so rugged through that part of the Sierra Madres, that The Emperor Maximilian used them for his redoubt, and Emiliano Zapata easily avoided capture by the Federal troops during Mexico's repeated revolutions. There was a folk song that said “It would be better for “El Colonel” (commander of the troops in pursuit of Zapata) to stay in his barracks, for Zapata is like a ghost who moves with the wind.”.

Descending the Eastern slope of the Sierras in the old Oldsmobile, with two flat tires, proved ultimately not to be possible. Not because of the tires, one could still move forward on rims, but because of the three rivers that had to be crossed. We got stuck in the first, but with a herculean effort managed to dig out and proceed. The second was wider and it was there we got stuck, around three AM with the moonlight illuminating the sparkling water. It was strangely peaceful. The problem was that we were blocking the only shallow place, and there were rustlers with a stolen bull coming up the mountain who needed to pass. They put us under guard and commandeered every farm truck in the vicinity (all three) and with long ropes, ingenuity and much effort supplied by nearly the entire nearby village, at gunpoint, they got the Old's up and out and proceeded up the mountain into the night, with the stolen bull on the back of their truck bellowing at the top of his lungs the entire time.

The next morning the entire village turned out again, this time not at gunpoint, and helped push the Olds up some planks onto the back of a cattle truck, which brought us across the third much wider and deeper third river and into Puerto Vallarta.

We rented a small house several blocks back from the beach with a walled garden and a huge mango tree for 65 dollars a month and settled into the exclusive movie colony isolated private paradise life style. PV in 64 was still a very small town. But was charming beyond belief. Pioneered by John Huston who brought cast and crew to PV to film Tennessee Williams “Night of the Iguana” in 63. At the time there was no airport, Just a short landing field. One public phone, and no road south of the town. Access to South seas paradise beach enclaves of Mismaloya, Boca de Tomatatlan, and totally unspoiled Jelapa was only by boat. For a brief period before being overrun it was a quiet haven for the Jet Set and a Movie Colony retreat.

One of the best friends I made at the time was John Drew Barrymore Jr. John was more fun than a barrel of puppies to hang out with. He could do all the trick riding stunts that you see in the movies and we galloped in a pack for many a mile. Body surfing and skin diving were popular. For 40 cents an hour the vaquero's son would leave horses tied outside in the morning. A ride to the beach a swim and breakfast in paradise was the healthiest and greatest life style I ever lived. Steve McQueen had a house there, and the only dog in town who could beat ours when out riding. John was there. John Wayne came in his yacht and tried to get Barrymore to come back to Hollywood. Elizabeth Taylor still had a house by the river connected by a romantic bridge to Richard Burton's. It was living in Paradise, with the happy beautiful people.

It was still legal in those days to import Mescaline from England, and LSD from Switzerland into Mexico. Especially if you established a "Research Laboratory". Also one could make organic Mescaline in a simple extraction process out of domestic peyote. That resulted in a wide variety of chemically pure psychedelics being available for experimentation. For the totally dedicated, solvent, and adventurous there were guided guru tours of the 8 varieties of mushrooms available on the third day of the rainy season only in one obscure village. The drugs were supposed to induce telekinetic powers, extrasensory experiences and exotic side effects. Not for the faint of heart.

I had a chance to practice the music that I had learned in Spain and began studying Indian music on tapes of Ravi Shankar from John's Limo. Being a resident Spanish guitarist meant that over several months all the other guitarist for many miles around came around to spend an afternoon under the mango tree in the courtyard, swapping chords and musical phrases. I made many friends among the mariachis.

A few months into the trip there was a spectacular evening at a restaurant. We were having a total blast. It was elaborate dinner party, at a long table, with John B, a Swedish actress friend of his, and several other glittering beautiful souls. We were all under the influence of low dosages of pure psychedelics and the laughter was continuous. The party was interrupted by a screaming angry man who found the sight of the happy group so offensive that he could not contain his rage. Stomping in place from foot to foot he denounced us with filthy language for several minutes until the management finally prevailed on him to leave. We all giggled throughout which just pissed him off more. It was my first encounter with The Narc who was later to be known as "The Villain"

After several months in country, I was walking down a path from an idyllic Beach house at the end of "Los Muertos" Beach in the old town of PV. I was contacted by a representative of some NY agency whom I had briefly met before during the Boston/Cambridge “Hootenannies”. While unsure of exactly who he worked for I knew he was connected with some high ranking enforcement people.

He was waiting by the path near the beach, and was pretending to fish. He said “hello”, and I asked him what he was doing there. He was there, he said, to “investigate the psychedelics” and that he had been appointed to “The New York State Narcotics Commission”. I pointed out that I doubted that they had much jurisdiction in PV, and besides he was fishing in the wrong spot. He said he was there with the “Director of Midwest Narcotics Enforcement based out of Chicago”. These guys didn't have a clue. I recommended they try the drugs before condemning them.

Agent Ghost said “whats the effects?” I said “they make you psychic” “for example,if you put your line right there you will catch a fish”, He did just to prove me wrong and to his complete shock he immediately hooked a huge 2 kilo bonito. I was just screwing with the guys mind, I knew from diving where the fish lived, and was glad when after a brief furious fight, the fish escaped. The agents were psyched out and hooked though.

Robert Graves, the Poet Laureate of England was a winter Resident and his mistress who was from Ibiza with French or Spanish citizenship was on the beach. She offered to give them each a dose of acid. Normal dose, pure Sandoz. One, the ghost, palmed the tab and faked taking the dose that she provided and tried to act high. The one from Chicago that did take the LSD wound up many hours later standing on a balcony railing, In a mega mansion, high above a crashing sea, conducting 11 mariachis, with a rose, naked, with the Lady from the Beach.

He left on the first plane in the morning. I heard somewhere that he quit his job. The other guy left too, but I would be seeing him again.

Immediately their began a period of intense scrutiny, which continued for months. First with Mexican Federales. An 18 man federal team in three shifts of 6 officers changing every 8 hours were dispatched from Mexico DF to PV at the request of the American Authorities and arrived about the time that everyone was packing and leaving. The guru packed up and left for LA, John left for Guadalajara and then Hollywood, The flock of jet setters dispersed as the summer came on. They 18 man team was busy. PV was a very small town. Fortunately they focused on the Drug Gurus circle of friends, and for a while we remained under the radar living quietly on the north side of town through the rainy season. But then it was late summer and we were getting ready to go north.

They followed our every move up to the border but we slipped through the net and out of the country. That’s a long and great story, one of life's great romantic memories and adventures. The completely fictional details are contained in the book “Hashmakers” available on Amazon.

MAKING RECORDS

Briefly we were harassed by local law enforcement on the US side who didn't believe we were US citizens until we dug out our passports and proved it. Even then the officer was suspicious. After a winter in the Casbah of Tangier and another in the sun and wild interior of Mexico we looked so bizarre , he said, "well iffen yew is US citizens then how come yew is carrying passports?" It was the last straw on a hot day for my GF and True Love. "And exactly what document do you suggest we carry to prove our citizenship?" she said in a voice dripping with NY sarcasm. The Officer took off and we were left alone to hitch to Taos in peace. We felt vulnerable until we dove deeper underground and arrived in Hollywood to hang with Barrymore and our other friends in LA from the PV community.

Traveling with a German Shepard, and dressed in a cross between north Africa and Mexican wild jungle, we attracted a lot of negative attention. We hitched from the border, to Taos, then by bus to La and Sunset boulevard.

They wouldn't allow the dog on the bus of course, so we went to a leather goods store, bought some handles, harness and straps, and made a "seeing eye dog harness" With dark glasses and my pretty companion guiding me the dog was believable until he picked fights with other males, snarled at policeman and anyone carrying a concealed gun, made friends, chased females, and worked the bus for handouts, all of which real seeing eye dogs don't do, but it was the only way to get him on a bus. This resulted in being followed by various local bunco and "fraud squad" units who assumed we were up to something, they just didn't know what.

About the time they were getting tired of observing and ready to pounce we were recognized by friends in a passing limo on Sunset boulevard and whisked away into the hills, leaving the local vice squad literally scratching their heads. John lived a furtive, energetic, "star fun" life. Always welcome, always celebrated, always interesting. We settled into the Malibu beach house and enjoyed the star entourage poolside life style with Tim Hardin, John and other members of the scene. Lost in the Hollywood hills, hanging out at Lenny Bruce's house, (after Lenny's death) Tim Hardin was living in Tom Law's house, John knew everybody. We went to the movie lots with John and his beautiful friend Nina Wayne who was the ingenue in a sitcom called "Camp

Runamuck". She was the twin sister of sister of Johnie Carson's muse Nina Wayne (the blond in his skits) The Wayne sisters were twin ice skating stars from the early 60's.

John B. was being groomed for a lead in a detective series, but I was advocating for a production of "Siddhartha". John was was rebelling against the conventional wisdom and was living the part of Siddhartha growing a wild beard and running through the brush in the high desert. We went to the beach, recorded with a friend of Steve McQueen's in Steve's studio, tried to get a group together, toured the Houdini Mansion, and took phone calls by the side of the pool in one of those huge apartment complexes in central Hollywood. We had shaken off the scrutiny and were once again anonymous, underground, and thus, we thought, safe. After a while in Malibu, we headed back east.

Leaving the West coast had been a strategic decision, There was no immediate musical future for me at that time there. My love and I missed the bookstores, coffee houses, and intellectual stimulation of Boston. We were low on money, and perhaps worse, we had attracted the scrutiny of an obsessive "super-groupie type", who was either an obsessive compulsive control freak, sociopathic stalker type, or was just a random total nut job or in the employ of some unknown entity, or agency. Regardless of which reality was true the harassment was unwelcome.

Any chance of doing a musical soundtrack for a film version of "Siddhartha" with John B. seemed unlikely because of the intense pressure to do the detective series deal. At one point we just got out of the limo and returned to normal life. Driving through the moonlit Rocky Mountains has always been a favorite. Once again, free, anonymous, in the wind, headed east.

Living in Cambridge, back on my "home turf" I played, practiced, studied, and somehow crossed that fine line between wanting to play and being a player.

I had "tried my wings" on the cross country trip a year befoe and had been well received. In Texas, Monterey, North Beach, the audiences liked what they heard, With the addition of the Indian Raga material and the studies in Spain and Mexico I had a "presentation" of material ready for audiences to hear and was eager to share the joy and delight of the musical fusions and discovery's which were unfolding in my musical life. I really had a lot more to learn, but was ready to start sharing what I had. Influenced by jamming on the East coast with Sandy Bull, and on the West coast with Perry Lederman, I started to perform in open tunings, switching off with poignant Spanish pieces.

Monty Dunn came up to Cambridge in April of 66, and we jammed together, several times. It was Monty who invited me to New York City and got me my first work doing rehearsals and sessions for Colombia. Playing in the "basket houses" of the Village at night, at one place at 4:AM Jose Feliciano would take his turn. Monty introduced me to a hard core life style of practicing all day every day, with other players. It is how it is done in Spain also. Stopping by Lance Wakeley's for an hour, then John Sebastian's, then Dave Bromberg's for an hour of super intense scales, chops, and mastery.

In the mornings at my hotel in the village, the day would start with an hour's practice with an Arabic Violin Player who was living "on the lam" down the hall. His name was "Al the Arab" and was wanted in Boston for something. I was familiar with the scales that he played so it made a good way to begin the day. To give you an idea, I went through a set of strings every day.

Between that, WBAI most nights all night, the basket houses, the sessions, the practice, it became a natural process to work all the time, to become a Union Local 802 member, and, finally, become a professional musician. Once I started at the Cafe Au Go Go, It became my home base, club, and job when I was in NY which was most of the time. My Managers (Elan Asc) paid for my room at the Chelsea. They were able to book odd corporate gigs and midtown fashion gigs that brought in steady income to my usual pick-up band without having to travel. The pick-up band was my usual studio session cronies that I practiced with anyway, and who played on "Rainy Day Raga" It was a stable happy life.

Over the next two years I was busy doing session work at Columbia and recording two albums, Rainy Day Raga and Second Poem for Vanguard. The norm became a bi-coastal life style between NY, LA and SF. Besides the ubiquitous anti-war concerts, and WBAI benefits there were no political activities to speak of, and aside from an interesting evening sharing my world and view point with Senator Kennedy I had no contact with politicians, agents, or agencies.

Just Tim Leary. I had known Tim since 62 and hung out at the Newton house while Tim was still at Harvard. I was impressed with his sharp mind. The experiments with LSD and divinity students, and the studies in reducing recidivism rates at Mass state prisons that were conducted at Harvard were very encouraging.

Up at Millbrook one weekend Tim found out one of the guests had some hash. Not a lot, about a finger, a few grams. Tim asked to see it and took it directly the toilet and flushed it. Given the recent raids it was the right thing to do, it was a good example from a great role model. I took note.

Tim was mercurially fluid in his intelligence and functionality. I rode into town with him once from Millbrook, wild from a weekend on a 4000 acre estate in the woods, we arrived near his destination on the upper East side, he reached behind the seat for a paper bag containing his Harvard professor uniform and emerged from the vw van in seconds transformed from wild guru to Harvard professor in a matter of moments, like superman emerging from the phone booth.

I think Tim chose me to play the music at the "Celebrations" because of the Eastern and Indian influence. The East West fusion fit in with his presentations. Also I was a known member of the original circle out of Cambridge. I had certainly paid my dues playing for perhaps hundreds of benefits, like the "Community Breast" concerts which I think funded the East Village Other, or one of a zillion other lower east side causes, like the Paradox Restaurant who fed the masses brown rice and fish for a dollar or so, and Earth Peoples Park who housed them. The East Village Other wrote in scathing terms about the war and the protests. When in the city I played all night on Bob Fass's "Radio Unnameable" with Monty Dunn.

I traveled regularly to do radio shows every several weeks from NYC to LA and SF.

At Ravi Shankars Kinnara School in LA and Ali Akbar Khan's School in Berkeley I sat at the feet of these masters and took, borrowed, and copied, copious notes. I was obsessed and delighted with access to the musical secrets off the orient. I still worked at the cafe Au go go, when in NY, but other work was falling off. Study was prevailing over playing, but still there was enough work to support the bi-coastal life style. My management screwed up a planned tour with the Maharishi and the Beach boys, I was treading water in the musical sense. I knew that I would need years to really digest what I had learned.

LEVEL THREE

THE ORIENT EXPRESS

It was 1967 In the fall. I had just returned from a summer in Berkeley California. Ali Akbar Khan had approached me at "The World Festival of Indian Music" produced by Ben Shapiro in the Hollywood Bowl. He literally tapped me on the shoulder and said, "Come to my school. I will teach you that which you are seeking". I left the next morning for Berkeley, hitchhiking while loaded with instruments and baggage. I spent the summer as a classmate of Sandy Bull's sister at the feet of "Khan Saab" (Pandit Khan Sahib). I was now the only Union professional musician in NYC with formal training in Indian Classical Music. I was friends with Ravi, had been to school with George Harrison, with a copy of Sandy's sister's notes in my bag I was ready for a new level of playing. My second Vanguard album was in the works.

Stanley Bard,was the manager of the Chelsea Hotel on 23rd Street in NYC, The Chelsea had been home base since I had hooked up with "Elan Associates", a fledgling artist management partnership that was handling Rudi Stern the light show Artist, a writer who was dating Judy Collins, and me. I later brought in Bob Mormon who founded "Elephants Memory".

I had moved from Room 104 which was a small room with a large bay window overlooking the rear yards of the houses on the next block. Because of my then level of artistic success I moved into a really great long room with a kitchenette, bay window with same view, and a small antique roll top writing desk. My father came to visit from Boston with his girlfriend, Lily Bodke, and was suitably impressed. Lily is worth a paragraph unto herself.

Lily was the widow of professor Irwin Bodky of Berlin and Brandies Universities. Prof. Bodke was the author of several books on the music of J.S. Bach and fled Germany when Hitler rose to power. He had become head of the music department at Brandeis where he had remained until his death. My Dad met Lily and they became life companions for the balance of Lily's lifetime. Each year they would take trips to Germany and deal with publishers who were translating Prof Bodky's books on Bach into many languages. They traveled in style and had many important baroque and classical music friends. It was through Lily that I met friends of Wanda Landowska and members of her elite classical peer group of harpsichordists, clavier players and early baroque music aficionados. As my father said "it was all grist for the mill" He was very pleased with my situation, and quoted from Tennyson's "Ode to intimations of immortality." With my regular gig at Howard Soloman's Cafe Au Go Go life was stable. Lily, my Dad and I had dinner at Max's Kansas city and celebrated my success.

When the phone on my desk rang in the fall of 67 I was blown away by who it was from and what they had to say. The person on the phone was told me that they were working for a man named Eddie Ticknor, who was partners with Jim Dixon, the producer of the Byrds. They said that they wanted to make me an offer, and would pay for a first class ticket and Hotel if I would fly out and talk to him.

I told them that I would get back to them later that day. I took the subway up to 57th street near Carnegie Hall, and talked to my manager at the time Ely Ask, from Elan Asc. He said go and see what they have say. So I called back, said yes, and headed for the airport.

At that time there was a VIP airlines club that was called the "quarter million mile club". It was in competition with American Airlines "Admirals Club". Since I had a first class ticket, (first time for me) I inquired at the ticket agent when I picked up my ticket and boarding pass about membership in the club. The ticket agent was a little dismissive. "that's only for people that have flown a quarter million miles on our airline" I was told. I said "but I have", and opened my briefcase to reveal a large stack of ticket stubs acquired over the last couple of years, that probably didn't total the actual number of miles required, but was pretty close. I knew that they weren't going to sift through them and count. It was a very thick bundle of tickets, mostly NY - SF, and NY - LA. The ticket agent was quite impressed, and became quit respectful, after all I was flying first class.

I got to my seat on the plane, front row left, and after takeoff, the Captain sent back an inquiry, "Was I the gentleman who had brought the tickets to prove that I had flown a quarter million miles on their airline?" I said "yes". What happened over the next few hours was literally the high point of my life. The captain altered his flight plan to go north of the Grand Canyon, and requested an altitude change to the planes functional ceiling, close to 65 thousand feet. Heading out over the US in a gentle curve. At that height the plane gently banked over the grand canyon, and I could see through the 1st class picture window the curvature of the earth. As close to space as I will ever get. That and the great food and too many drinks from the attentive, hot stewardess made it the most memorable flying experience ever.

It was a roller coaster of a ride, which continued after I landed, took a cab to Hollywood and settled into a Hotel in the eight thousand block of Sunset, across form the "Whiskey Au Go Go." and just a couple blocks from the 9000 building at the Beverly Hills line which housed Jim Dixon and Ed Ticknor's office. By incredible stroke of fortune Barrymore was staying at the same place. My LA contact from Ticknor's office was living in a charming English Tudor town house on Larrabee a couple blocks away.

The next morning at the Dixon/Tickner office at the 9000 building Eddie Ticknor explained the deal. He had taken a copy of my album Rainy Day Raga, taped white paper around it so that the front and back covers were completely concealed and gone to 1st a record company, and then to a publisher. His proposal to them was; upon their hearing the record, whether they would advance 25,000 dollars each towards the production of a group produced by the author of the album they were listening to. They both said yes. So, the proposal to me was not could I lead, produce and play in such a group? But would I?.

The temptation of a pop music product and a $50,000.00 dollar budget was beyond too much. Despite my stable life and career in NYC, I was unable to refuse. Within a few hours I had a brand new mustang convertible, (Leased) and was out shopping for a rental among the mansions of Hollywood. Within a couple days I was ensconced in a large Mulhulland Drive house with large pool and stunning views of the LA basin below. It was the top of the “Hollywood Hills”. In the words of Lord Buckley “It was so far uptown one could get a nose bleed” Too bad it wasn't fated to last long, but that too is Hollywood. It quickly became a scene of it's own, with instruments, visiting musicians, ladies and friends. I remember throwing a trespassing reporter into the pool. It was a struggle to ride herd on it all.

Initially I had a large budget, and a free hand. The first problem was to select the musicians.

My prime players from NYC were Monty Dunn (perhaps the greatest steel string guitarist that ever lived) and Bruce Langhorne. Monty had become totally wrapped up in his relationship and musical partnership with his then girl friend, and was writing and singing fabulous stuff, but was definitely not available. Bruce was busy with sessions and albums and hadn’t made the move to LA yet. I got in touch with Lowell George. We hung out and played some and he was a perfect choice, competent and intent.

My very first choice, however was Judy Mayhen. It went back to one of the Tim Leary psychedelic Celebrations back at the Village Theater. It was the third or fourth week. Each performance had been JAM Packed to the rafters. Thousands of people, it was a huge theater. Since I had a small budget for the opening music, I was spreading it around among musicians who need the work and opportunity. Monty Dunn was my playing partner at the time. Except for the the Au Go Go, I wouldn’t do a gig without him. He had invited me to NY after jamming with me several times in Boston in early 66, and got me my first studio gigs, He guided me through many of the pitfalls of the industry, made sure I got into the Union and was my best friend. He suggested one night just before show time, that I go and get Judy Mahen to do a number. I had no idea who she was, but I absolutely trusted Monte's musical judgment. I took a cab over to Mott Street in the west village and climbed the stairs to a fifth floor walk-up. The moment was particularly memorable because I had once briefly lived in the same apartment in 1966. Sleeping on a mattress on the floor was Judy Mahen, dressed in a plain green cotton house-dress.

She woke up, rubbed her eyes with her knuckles like a child, and in a sleepy voice asked what I wanted. I explained that Monty had asked me to to come get her and that we had a full theater of people that wanted to hear her sing. There was also a small stipend. She said "sure". I said "great I'll carry your instrument". She said "no instrument". I really wasn't too sure. From outward appearances, I didn't know what to expect. We took a cab back to the Village Theater. We arrived with about five minutes to spare, the house was packed, and it was time to start the show. I asked Judy, "do you need an instrument?, there are some great guitars here". She shook her head, she seemed to be concentrating. " Well how about a mike, where do you want the mike?", "no mike" she said. I turned to Monte, "are you sure?" I was really hesitant. If it was a totally bad decision I would be out of a great gig.
"I'm sure" said Monte who nodded his head. The moment was there. It was time. Judy mounted the few steps to the stage and walked up close to the apron. There was a sea of faces before her, thousands of people, hushed, waiting, expectant.

Judy began to sing. In a voice like liquid gold. It poured over the audience. She sang "he's got the whole world in his hands". She sang slowly, in round whole tones, filled with passion and palpable restrained power. At the end of the first verse the crowd was shocked and stunned. Judy began the second verse with a growing surety and upped the amps on the vocal power. Each verse became stronger and more liquid. She transcended, she captivated,. It was love. It was magic. By the time she reached the end of the song, this small lady, wrapped in a green house dress, unaccompanied, unamplified, brought these thousands of people to their feet in wild acclamation. I have had the privilege of witnessing thousands of great moments in music, but that was the greatest of all.

I wanted Judy for this group, and the great news is that she was living in LA. I went by to see her and she said "sure". She was a perfect choice and she had some great material to contribute.

So now I had Judy Mayhen, Lowell George, and I quickly recruited Maryvon who was a local amateur veena player, that only left percussion. There's where I made my biggest mistake. Deciding to import drum talent from Ali Akbar College in Marin county north of San Francisco might have been a good idea in theory but in practice it completely blew the budget. The costs of air fares, housing, payments, expenses, were all completely out of proportion to the net benefit.

We went into rehearsal in a rented (like everything in Hollywood) rehearsal space, with rented sound equipment, and spent a few weeks putting together a set of tunes for a gig. The goal was to be ready for a concert at Hollywood High which would be a benefit for the "Diggers Association" and would be the launching of the group. The Beatles press agent was enlisted to do the pre-concert press. What could go wrong???

Ok; lets start with the working name of the group. At some point it was discovered that some other group had called itself "The Orient Express". And the legal beagles were afraid of infringement, so we had to go look for another name. This led to some interesting dissent, but it was the first of many, many dissents. The three professionals were Judy, Lowell and I. The others were total amateurs who had never performed before, and it showed. The cost of importing the two students (and their family's) and flying them in on a weekly basis from San Francisco became impossible. Some of the nonessential band members didn't get along, but worst of all Eddie Ticknor pulled the plug. He just didn't see enough progress, and the expenses he was fronting became too much. He didn't feel he was going to be able to recoup and the demands, especially from the students, were too much.

In a card game its called knowing when to fold em. Eddie was occupied in negotiating the successful sale of "Up Up and Away by Jim Webb to American Airlines and had Jim's McArthur Park album finished and in the can ready to go for England for Richard Harris's voice overdub that would sell a million copies. He didn't need to be involved in an unwieldy project of doubtful outcome. After a total of several weeks the ride was over.

Apart from "groupie" problems, the student musician thing had killed the deal. If I had found a local drummer, if I hadn't thrown the reporter in the pool, if I hadn't been under contract to Vanguard, if I was older, wiser, and more mature, if if if. Nevertheless a deal was a deal, so we went on to perform at the "Hollywood High Benefit Concert for the Diggers", but without the backing and planning, and support in place it was just another gig. After the one and only public appearance of "The Fabulous Flipped Out No Names". We all went our separate ways. The students went back to SF, The amateur drone player went to England with Jim Webb and Ed Ticknor on the "MacArthur Park" album project. Lowell, Maryvon, and Judy just went home. I gave up the house on Mulhullond with the pool, put my Tamboura and most of my gear into storage, and returned to NY.

The Biafra Campaign

I flew back to NY with my guitar and a bag, moved back into the Chelsea, and resumed working at the Au Go Go. I also produced Ali Akbar Khan in Symphony Hall in Boston. This brought in a few bucks. It also brought me together with my Lady from the songs and adventures for the occasion. The reunion was brief but significant. Through my management (Elan) I got a deal writing an instruction book for the Coral electric sitar. The deal included expenses for a place to write so I flew back out to LA, bought a used Corvair Monza Spider and shared a house with Fred Tackett, (Dylan's band leader) and Julie Coryell, (then Julie Samuels) in Laurel canyon.

I was interested in a reconciliation with my ex from the Mexican/Africa/Spanish days but although we would briefly spend time together we could not hook up again. Maybe if we had gone away together, but we didn't. If if if. Maybe we still had more to learn, see, and do before we could be together again. Maybe we were just being typical young people from our age and era.

I returned to NY on June 5th, 1968.

When Bobby Kennedy was killed on June 6th I was staying in the 70's on the upper west side in Larry Coryell's old apartment. Larry had recently married Julie. I played for the wedding and had shared a house with Julie in LA when she met Larry. Because they were planning to live in Connecticut his apartment had become available.

In response to Bobby's death I became more political.

I had been in LA the day before, on June 5th, and was shocked beyond belief. I began looking for an outlet for the rage and pain. Because I was living uptown, (unusual for me) I went to or played for a demonstration at the UN and became became involved in the Biafra campaign. This involvement developed into "The Airlift To Biafra". It was an adventure worthy of it's own book.

The short version is that through an old friend from Boston, I wound up living in the “Jacques Lowe Loft” in NYC. At that time all of the official photos of the JFK administration were kept in a two story loft on 6th Avenue in what previously had been the residence of Jacques Lowe who had been the Bovier family photographer prior to the JFK administration and who had been the official photographer during the JFK Administration. Jacques had fled to France shortly after John's assassination, but had left 1000's of copies of the various photos taken before and during JFK's tenure. The loft and photos had been under the protection of a serious group of gentleman from Brooklyn. When I took occupancy in august 68 it was still under the constant supervision and scrutiny of da boys from Brooklyn.

The history of the loyalties of the friends of the Kennedy Family was/is unknown to me but included some passionate, loyal, and obviously very "heavy" gentleman, who never presented badges or ID but acted with an unmistakable air of authority and confidence.

I didn't know exactly who they were, but they definitely were in charge. One of their immediate associates had been a previous tenant, and was currently then out of the country on a long term sabbatical. Something about a Federal Warrant for Utilizing Jacques Lowe's Photographic Equipment to produce a photographic master printing plate of a government bond. Never a dull moment.

I did not know then that the building was also under the surveillance of several city, state, and federal agencies. Not all of whom had the same political interest or agenda or were working together in the same direction.

These included the original and mysterious agent from Boston, from 63 who had appeared in Mexico and had faked taking LSD in '65 (and who's agency was never identified by me), AKA "the ghost".

Some of Bobby's intelligent, noble and benevolent "young turks", who were still employed by the justice Department AKA "the heroes".

A really mean spirited violent crooked narcotics agent (the same one who had thrown the "hissy fit" as the dinner party in Mexico in 65) who's mission or assignment in life was to put me in jail, or at least put a stop to my activities who reported directly to Harry J. Anslinger,_who reported directly to Nixon in what was then the Chain of Command of what was then called "The Federal Bureau of Narcotics". AKA "the villain".

And an assortment of unidentified others from both sides of the law.

Each of the thousands of huge enlargement photos in high res were stamped on the back with the white house seal and were under the protection and jurisdiction of the Secret Service division of the Treasury Department as "White House Property". They were all destined for the Kennedy Library in Boston, but not until years later.

The photos were in stacks and sequences, showing meetings and reactions of participants, for example there was a second by second record of the deal with Lyndon for VP. It requires a expert to identify many of the people but there were hundreds of copies of certain sequences that were significant, in Lowe's opinion.

Da boys from Brooklyn stopped by once a week, usually someone well dressed and extremely intelligent accompanied by someone who dragged their knuckles as they walked. I was assured of their benevolence and protection, but was warned not to get "cute". The crooked Narc claimed he was in business with these guys. They kept track of the photo inventory by measuring the heights of the stacks with a yardstick. It took a while. Sometimes the piles got moved but the total line footage had to come out right.

Besides my prior activities maybe part of what landed me in that loft at that moment had to do with a counter intelligence operation that had been mounted a few months before at the beginning of the Biafran Campaign, and before one of the million man anti war marches in Washington. I was at a meeting with the anti-war movement representatives to coordinate the Biafran campaign with the anti-war movement, which had many political implications and broadened the support base. Senator Kennedy's office was in favor of this coalition.

The Biafran campaign civil war involved genocide of the Ibo tribes-people by the dominant and resentful Hausa Nigerians. Traditionally the Ibo had been the administrators and now wanted their own country because of atrocity's and repression by the Housas, thus the Biafran conflict came into being with thousands of children starving with staggering suffering in abundance. The very existence of such a scene was an atrocity. Film was being smuggled out by Peace Core workers.

The short term solution was to deliver food and medicine, and the long term solution was for the Ibo's to have a homeland. At the end of the campaign the Ibo's lost the civil war but were aided by Catholic relief in staging a coup in neighboring Gabon resulting in a homeland. RUMOR has it that the movie "Dogs of War" tells the story of that coup or one just like it. ;)

I had the great honor of receiving signed copies of three books on the subject of the conflict written by General Ojukyu, commander of the Biafran Forces, in recognition of my efforts on their behalf. I still have a Biafran Flag drawn by a Biafran Child who was saved by our efforts. Small treasures.

The US Peace Movement Leaders complained that all over the country the organizations and meetings were being penetrated and diverted by new members who advocated violence and who invariably turned out to be police who were disrupting a peaceful movement with violent advocacy and actions.

I suggested a solution. Since they knew their telephones were tapped, they should start talking in hushed tones about a new super secret super violent branch of the movement. Called “the crazies”. That way they could identify the police among the new applicants to join the various movement groups. Anyone who tried to identify themselves as being part of or affiliated with the non-existent “crazies” would obviously be lying, and therefore would be an undercover violence advocating cop or other undesirable.

It was incredibly successful, the “threat of the crazies” was taken seriously and budgets were inflated as agents and agency's fought for budget shares to counter this threat and establish a presence within it's ranks. A cross between a keystone cops episode and a Chinese fire drill.

That summer I was on my way through the mass of people in DC to play harmonica on the main stage with some of the cast from “Hair”. It was at one of the million man marches in DC against the war, (they should have been called gas-ins) and there were two obvious police undercover officers fist-fighting in a circle over who was the genuine “crazy”.

Even as late as the Woodstock Festival some undercover officer set up a booth for the “crazies”. It was an open secret by then and was comical. One of them even wrote a book about his “exploits”.

None of this, or the previous encounter in Mexico, had endeared me to the Narcotics fellow, (The Villain) who knew that I associated with a lot of friends in Hollywood and the NY music scene. He was hot to comb my address book for famous subjects to investigate but had no idea who was who. I told him to piss off. He was determined to bend or break my fingers or the rules to bring down his quarry but in reality he really wasn't very smart, so since I was in regular contact with Senator Kennedy's office I felt safe in resisting his obvious overtures and escalating threats.

I received the following explanation from the Justice guys who rescued me from this wacko, after I flushed down the toilet (thank you Tim Leary) an ounce of heroin this agent nut job had planted in my office.

The “Turks” explained that low level “bottom of the barrel” Feds like the guy that was harassing me were hard to get rid of because of civil service regulations and constraints.

They explained that there were guys who used their civil service office and equipment for surveillance, and then rob the subjects of their investigations, sell them their freedom, confiscate the drugs and money, sell the drugs to organized criminals, and keep the money . It was and probably still is going on worldwide in law enforcement, leaving the noble, idealistic, and fortunately higher ranking, federals to try and clean up their messes, and prosecute their accesses. .

During my several months at the Loft the adventures were constant, bizarre, and not really very believable. I have memories of volunteer CIA pilots spreading detailed aerial maps on the carpeted floor of the large front office They were reviewing blowups of sections of the African coast line plotting evasive air tactics. The flight into Biafra from Fernando Po Island required flying over Nigerian surface-to-air missiles.

Staging a support and maintenance facility on Fernando Po (Island off the west coast of Africa) required access to classified TO&E documents for equipment and supplies. State Department aircraft specialists were importuned by wealthy supporters to disclose information and provide logistical advice.

The theoretical “price per pound” of delivery of food to the starving children of Biafra dropped to around 2 – 3 cents a pound using huge CI30 pallet dropping techniques on short runways. The Nixon administration had no response to Senator Kennedy's evening national news conferences presenting flow charts and projection sheets (drafted by yours truly in the loft) proving the entire crisis was due to the Nixon administrations willful inaction. While the war raged and the bombs fell in Vietnam and Cambodia the bloated belly’s of the starving children appearing on national television were an ongoing embarrassment to the administration.

Senator Kennedy was relentless with his TV press conferences making the case for Nixon's callous indifference to the plight of the starving children while escalating the war. We drafted actual plans for both small and large scale food deliveries, and donated over 22.000 dollars to Catholic Relief and World council of Churches relief efforts.

I remember being told by a formal representative of the Nigerian government Secret Service, on a lonely west coast street corner, isolated, after going through several “cut-outs”, to attend the meeting, that they thought I was a well motivated fellow who should stay out of the national politics of another country if I enjoyed living. It was obvious, he pointed out, that I was vulnerable.

Memories and Fragments

I remember flying in a small plane in Central Mexico, following railroad tracks, looking for a trail in a desolate desert with alkali pools, dead animals rotting and vultures perched. I was searching for caves I had discovered years before full of bat guano, that could be used as flower fertilizer by the flower growers of Monterrey county in central California and finance the movement.

I remember driving in the Mexican jungle, checking out ranches and growers, looking for bee's wax that had soared to 6 - 8 $ a pound for use in cosmetics to raise money for the same purpose.

I remember flying over a mountain range in an attempt to reach a wealthy supporters ranch in Arizona, in a light plane piloted by a former (he said) CIA person, and discovering in a sudden downdraft that my seat wasn't bolted to the floor. We were lucky to get back on the ground in a stiff crosswind. I decided to drive.

I remember the Narc turning purple with rage and waving his gun at me for flushing his valuable ounce of heroin while the Justice guys (the heroes) pounded up the stairs to my rescue. They took the narc into the front office while I waited in the hallway, you could hear the yelling for a block. They shouted him down, pulled rank and told him to back off or be prosecuted.

I found out at some point that every visitor who took any of the pictures, (there were some) was followed and prosecuted for “theft of white house property”. Some were “turned” in ongoing investigations into Bobby's demise etc.

There were light moments, like the time my ex-girlfriend and true love hid under my desk while somebody stormed in over something gone bad between them. I never knew the exact details, but the person was NOT happy. My loyalties were clear, and I said that I hadn't seen her.

When the same true love was in the hospital and anxious late at night before an operation, I visited after hours by changing into a bathrobe in a hospital phone booth, and while pretending to be a lost patient, I gave them her room number. We played honeymoon bridge. It was another stitch in the fabric of love.

Sal Mineo became a friend for a while . He and the Hells Angels were tight. I was invited to the clubhouse. Now THAT was interesting.

I remember being kidnapped and held for several hours, at a private estate in Duchess county, by the Narc, allegedly to save my life after I pissed off some mob lawyer thug, (guilty) while they "negotiated a settlement" to a dispute over the lease at the loft.

The narc's (the villain) eyes bulged as he blurted to the justice department guys (the heroes) that he had complete knowledge of my "plot to bomb the Nixon-Eisenhower wedding" with "Rabid Bat Guano" from my "caves in Mexico", using "2nd hand WW2 fighter bombers from Arizona." He wanted a huge budget authorization to investigate and prosecute the "plot". (those darn crazies must have been at it again)

The Justice guys (the heroes) told him he needed to learn to differentiate between cynical humor and terrorist plotting. They apologized to me on behalf of the federal government for his having planted the ounce of heroin.

I remember the wonderful feeling when I called to Children s Hospital in Boston to ask for a donation of a plane load of medical supplies for Abbey Nathen's humanitarian relief flight to Biafra, and the director telling me to send a truck over from Logan airport and they would pack the plane. To actually get some relief through was immensely satisfying.

I flew to LA at one point during that Loft period, looking for confirmation of some scrap of information which I found, but had guns pointed at me and was told to stay out of the Bobby Kennedy investigation. The context was that I had tried to talk someone into returning some photos they had taken, just as mementos they claimed, explaining the consequences from both sides of the law. Shortly later gangster friends of theirs threatened me, I didn't go back to LA after that, for many years.

Time has dimmed many memories, and the fragments and insights of many memories are somewhat unreliable, yet time is revealing much of what must have been true. in regard to Jack, Bobby, Martin, Medgar. Oliver Stone got it pretty right about JFK, and the Bobby story is still emerging.

I have to say that at the end of the day it was a lot for a musician, who meant well but who was spending so much time administrating and evading that I wasn't working. I moved out of the loft and back into the Chelsea Hotel, which had been home base through most of the 60's.

Janice was living at the Chelsea, Arthur Miller still stayed there. Every band who came through New York stayed there and it was a thriving throbbing hotbed of activity.

I had lived there from 66 on and kept a room on the 2nd floor with a kitchenette and bay window. The Chelsea was home base for nearly 5 years. The rent on the corner room was 27 dollars a week. The larger unit with kitchenette was $125 per month. My management paid the bill, and deducted the cost from my pay doing midtown shows for corporate and fashion evens almost always with the same musicians from Rainy Day Raga. . Ken Keasy's bus would pull up when in town and the party would go on for a day or so up on the roof.

One of my favorites stories from the Chelsea came one morning shortly after I resumed residence there from the Lowe Loft. I had a meeting in the Lobby with a couple representatives of some group who wanted to assist in putting together a "telethon" for Biafra. They were in the act of telling me that I was a liar and had no ability to bring in the kind of top name talent that would be required to make it a success. At that precise moment the elevator door opened. Janice sashayed out into the Lobby in full regalia, wide floppy hat and all. She stopped and turned to the seated group in the lobby. "Peter honey, you just tell me when your ready to do that telethon, and I'll be right there for ya." she turned and sailed out the door. The look on the faces of the naysayers was priceless. One stammered "was that um is that I mean was that … I said "yup"

Janice did a concert at the Fillmore East that stands out in my mind as one of the greatest I had ever seen. The Fillmore East was in the old East Village theater where the Timothy Leary "Celebrations" were held. It was a very large venue and was packed to the rafters. Janice and the band did their entire repertoire, it was nearly 2:30 am. The audience was nuts for more. Janice said, "that's all we have, but I tell you what, we can do it all again for ya" They did, the audience cheered through every note, went on till 5 AM. It was great.

I liked hanging out with her at the Chelsea. She was friendly as a puppy, and twice as sweet. It was the drinking that spoiled it. At one point I was asked by her management if I would be her road manager. It paid 350 a week which was a lot off money then, but I said no, The drinking was a turn-off, and I had my own music to do.

When the Narc continued to pursue and threatened to throw me out of an 8 story window of the presidential suite of the Chelsea, while I was in the middle of working two phone lines organizing support amongst the movie community for Senator

Kennedy's "Americans for Biafran Relief" coalition being announced that week with a huge press conference in DC, I definitely wanted out. It was like the road runner v. Wylie E Coyote, but I had had more than enough.

My music industry lawyer at the time was Hy Shore, a literal one armed bandit Attorney who represented, or at least sympathized with the peripheral elements of the music industry, hoping for a big win one day that never came. Almost assuredly because of his own terrible reputation for dishonesty, bad faith, and theft. But he was still a member of the bar who after all was an officer of the court and had some big time mob connections of his own. He was a sleazy character but was the only one I could afford, He was negotiating the contract of the cartoon movie deal. He talked some sense into the Narc or at least assured him that he couldn't bodily harm me with impunity.

I appeared at the Press conference in Washington, received recognition from Sen. Kennedy for my work as one of the founders, of "Americans for Biafran Relief" and returned to NY. I had been earning "bread and butter" money doing script synopsis writing projects for a film company and location shooting with a camera rig for the same film maker, (Ed Mann).

I finished up a movie deal with William Morris involving a friends script for the animated cartoon asap and with my share of the proceeds went to Marin County north of SF. It was easy to dive underground and blend into the redwood trees for an interlude of peace and music. California country roads, sunshine, horses, and friends were good medicine.

I flew back East for the Woodstock Festival. From there I retreated to an obscure small apartment on the lower east side and began to perform and record again in NY and Michigan. I met Eugene Skuratowicz backstage at the Woodstock Festival. He was managing canned heat at the time. He became my manager for a while, we remained friends and he is my manager now.

The Album, "Has anybody seen our freedoms?" is of the songs that I sang and the guitar music that I performed for hundreds of thousands of people and played on the air at the time. I wrote the original lead sheets on the back of guitar cases and on the red-eye back and forth between LA, SF, and Detroit. And were truly a snapshot in time of my soul. The anti-war movement coalition was a success. After the end of the war was announced the coalition could not agree on a new agenda, and disbanded. In many ways this album represents my requiem for the 60's. Its what I have to say.

After a year or so shuttling between NY and Detroit I moved to Woodstock where I have maintained a home base while continuing to travel, study, practice, grow, and enjoy the wonderful adventure of life. Lord Buckley would have said that I was "blown out onto the cool sweet sands of serenity".

THE CAMPER KING

Moving to Woodstock was a spiritual godsend. In the tranquility and peace of the country life I have had years of time to study the Indian raga sheet music from school, practice the Spanish guitar, raise kids and live a healthy rural life. The first benefit of Woodstock was that I spent the next ten years working for Ron Marions as a house musician for the "Joyous Lake" in Woodstock, in much the way that I was the House musician and opening act for the "Cafe Au Go Go" during the mid 60's I had a home musical base. Everybody I knew from the city passed through. Woodstock was and is a popular weekend destination for NY City dwellers and many keep a second home there. I had visited during the 60's but now I was a full time resident.

Billy Mitchel was a little known but genuinely talented singer songwriter at the time with one Mercury album. Billy had left an old pickup sinking into the mud in some field and had gone back to the city. I saw him one weekend shortly after my arrival and asked him if I could have it. He said sure. After inflating four tires, changing a starter motor and installing battery, I was mobile, and because I had the pickup truck I was instantly employed. Ron Marions paid 30 dollars a week for me to play on weekends, and the rest of the time I was free to move things, collect things, haul trash, building materials, and all the various odd jobs that accrue to the owner of a pickup truck in a small town more than half occupied by city folk.

They always needed something, fire wood, a piano moved, pieces of a burnt out house taken to the dump. It was instant employment. It was freedom from the pollution, drugs, and crime of the city. I have to say that driving down a country road in a pickup with my dog and I both enjoying the fresh country air was a high like none other. I was due to go back to the city. I decided to stay in the country.

I had a dog that I had acquired in the city from a Native American gentleman. While living on East 4th Street on the lower east side, I chanced upon a fellow who was sleeping in the hallway of a friends apartment building on 1st street. . He had a dog that he had found on the street. He told me that he was dying, and that he would give me the dog if I would take him to live in the country. In keeping my promise I believe that it saved my life. I really had no place to return to in the city. The junkies had overrun my building on East 4th street.

In Woodstock one of my best friends was Robert Dacey. Bob's art had been on the cover of "Life:, and he was a cutting edge psychedelic artist. Through a friend of Bob's I rented a 10,000 square foot factory building in the nearby town of Saugerties. In between playing at "the Lake" and odd jobs with the pickup, I went to work constructing a working model of a camper design that I had been working on ever since the cross country trip through Dallas in 1964.

They say that necessity is the mother of invention, and it's true. The motivation and inspiration for my camper design came from that trip. Driving a tiny Morris Minor across country was a great way to save on gas, it got more than 60 miles to the gallon, but the tiny space was torture. It was nifty and nimble, a friend called it "The marvelous Morris Minor, the modern mechanized marvel of the machine age". It was a very cool car, but very small. As the thousands of miles rolled by one could not help but think of a bigger vehicle, with more space, and what form it would take.

Conventional "campers" were bulky and heavy. I wanted something light and expandable. I was intrigued with the idea of a camper design that was smaller while traveling but would expand when parked. Finally in 1971 in Woodstock I had a chance to implement the ideas into a working model. My friend Dacey had built a charming cabin on a friends property which was quite habitable. The total materials cost had been under 500 dollars. (1971 prices). over the next 14 years I would build seven campers, and motor homes.

A few people even called me "The Camper King". It was a fun life style. Primitive, but fun. I began to experiment with heat exchangers and wind generators. I put a coil inside the stovepipe of a tiny wood-stove and reclaimed the waste heat energy as hot water. The stored hot water would heat the camper long after the fire had burned out. We were comfy and warm in blizzards and wind chills down to fifty below. Road testing the various models was a blast, all over the Northeast, throughout the South West, California, as far as the high desert of central Mexico, and camping on the wild west coast south of Puerto Vallarta.

Building the campers allowed me time, free from the hassle of generating money for rent and expenses, airfares, taxis, bills. The life style required very little cash. It also allowed unlimited time for practice, and after the turbulent years of the 60's, for healing.

It took years to practice and absorb the material in my notes from school, and years more to acquire the physical skills that would enable me to raise a family. I still played at "the Lake" but only once a week, on Sunday mornings for four hours. I practiced the

Indian Ragas from the Sanskrit school notes using the steering wheel of a bread truck for a music stand and slowly absorbed the material. I had a local following of people that liked my music, and an occasional student, but I was definitely off the national stage, and enjoyed my "retirement" from the Federal lime light with its attendant and obvious problems.

This interlude of relative tranquility lasted from 1971 until 1985 when I moved back to NYC for 15 years first to go back to School at Baruch and then under the supervision of an attorney and law partner, I practiced law for 15 years before returning to Woodstock in 2000. These were the interesting and adventure filled "long lost years" during which I practiced daily, and lived a hundred other lifetimes.

Appendix: Raga sheet music, kinartic scales and explanations.

LEVEL FOUR

My own personal musical Nirvana

The great musical adventure began again in 2000. With the turn of the century I lost my mother to old age, and after paying bills etc inherited a little money I also come down with prostate cancer.

It was a big time wake up call. It was time to think about life goals , and bucket lists. I had been gone from the Music Industry for 30 years. I wasn't thinking music business at all, I just wanted to learn more about the guitar and gain a better understanding of how to play this instrument that had been so much a part of my life. In a sense I just wanted to complete my education, and if not then then when? I flew to Spain.

I knew from my visits and studies in the early 60's, and a trip to Madrid in the mid 70's that Valencia had a limited Flamenco community, and that the Madrid music scene was huge, dangerous, very private, and scattered. Most of the Flamenco World and community is screened and protected from "Payo" (non-gypsy) intruders. Hanging out in the wrong place or at the wrong time could definitely get you assaulted or stabbed, by a remarkably large, (foot long blade) and razor sharp folding knife. The Gypsy culture is knife oriented and some of the greatest singers in a neighborhood are among some of the most dangerous residents. It is no wonder that many of the greatest bull fighters come from gypsy families. Fear doesn't exist when they are caught up in passion. For some, their skills with a knife are as amazing as their skills with a guitar, or song, or dance. Many of the finest fighters in the Flemish Wars were from the gypsy families and were granted papers which exempted them from the expulsions and genocides that were practiced upon the Gypsy population of the late 17th century.

It was in Granada in 1829 that the word Flamenco Music was first coined. It happened like this: Washington Irving resided in The Alhambra for an interlude in 1829. While there he could hear from his balcony the music of the Calo Gypsies across the arroyo from the castle in the Sacromonte neighborhood a few hundred yards away. He found it enchanting and asked "what it was" He was told that it was the music of "Los Flamencos". What that meant was that the music was being played by the residents of the Sacromonte who were called "Flamencos" because they held papers that exempted them from the anti gypsy expulsions and enslavement's because of the service of family members in the Flemish wars that Spain was engaged in at the time. In return for the service of the adult males the families were exempted from genocidal-like round-ups, and allowed to remain in their traditional (since the late 8th century) homes. When Irving wrote about his experiences in Spain he exalted the fabulous "Flamenco Music" and the name stuck.

The rest of the Spanish population (95%) resent the obvious fact that the Gypsies are the true soul of Spain and besides sherry are their only major export product. Modern Flamenco is subsidized by the government with a 10 percent tax on corporate profits going to the arts. This finances all the dance companies that tour the world representing "Spanish Culture" It is Ironic that in their home country they are derided discriminated against and generally shunned and mistreated by a majority of the population. There are reasons for some of this animosity.

The true Spanish Gypsy is a very special person. They are called Calo's and speak a Sanskrit based language, which is a mixture of 8th Century Indian Sanskrit from Bengal and Madras, mixed with many Arabic, and Spanish words. It is not the same language as spoken by the Romany gypsies who arrived on the Iberian peninsula late in the 17th century, although the two groups can understand each other.

Unlike the Romanies The Calo's had been brought to Spain by the Moors in the late eight century as "prizes of war" They had been selected for export from Bengal and Madras shortly after the Moorish conquest of India, and had been selected for their talent, beauty, bravery, or skills. Many had been entertainers at the conquered courts. . The greatest talent and the most beautiful woman of India had been brought to the Sacromonte neighborhoods above the city of Granada to serve the Royal court at the Alhambra. There were oral traditions within the some of the Calo families to "Never forget, that they are the long lost children of Madras and Bengal".

It was in the 17th century with the arrival of the Roma's, that problems arose for the acculturated Calos, who were also called "Gitanos de Casa" or gypsies who lived in houses (As opposed to the nomadic Roma). The difference between the two groups was incredible, On one hand the Calos were established integrated, talented and secure. The Roma's changed all that, they weren't prizes of war or especially talented artists or craftsmen, they were for the most part a wave of impoverished and not particularly talented immigrants from Northern India and Pakistan, traveling east over the north of the Mediterranean picking up every vagrant criminal and misfit along the way. The route is documented in the Movie "Lacho Drom"" and their arrival spelled doom to the peaceful Calos. After not many years of wholesale theft and overrunning of the rich fields and farms of Spain, The Spanish Government cracked down on all gypsies. They were rounded up and sent off to slavery in the eastern mines.

The Alhambra is an Acropolis like mini City State that was built on a promontory jutting out from the foothills of the incredibly rugged Alhapurras mountain range and gave it a impregnable command of the entire Spanish plain below. Below is the present day city of Granada. Opposite the castle ascending the hill to the right of the castle complex (it's huge) is first the dreaded "Albaizin Arabic neighborhood, parts of which really do deserve their reputation, and above that is the gypsy neighborhood, or barrio called the "Sacromonte" (sacred mountain). ALL of the guide books advise to stay away and that you will be hounded robbed scammed fleeced and chased. (none of this was true, but you still had to use basic common sense, and always be courtiers, don't wear sneakers) The sides of the all the hills in the area are honeycombed with Caves dating back to Neanderthal times. In most cases as the city expanded houses were built over the caves with ascending terraces and stunning views of the castle. The present day gypsies of the "Sacromonte" have some of the best real estate in Europe.

Up until the 17th century the Calos had a good thing going, on one level. They were a small group but they were a big influence, and had a certain degree of autonomy.

With the arrival of Ferdinand and Isabella in 1492 at the time of the "reconquesta" (re-conquering) they were liberated from their status as prizes of war and slaves. The Famous "Reconquesta" wasn't quite what it seemed. Yes it was true that The Alhambra was the last major strong point to fall back into Christian hands, but the terms of the surrender were actually quite favorable to the Moors, and left them with the southern slopes of the Alhapurras as their "fief" and the terms of the peace agreement gave the moors free rights to come and go, Also the Alhapurras were as defensible in their own way as the Alhambra had been, The Moors continued to be a problem in Spain for the next few hundred years. They would raid the lowlands from the mountain strongholds. And were impervious to counter measures, because of the incredibly rough terrain and narrow passes.

The key element in ousting the Moors from the impregnable Alhambra was a deal struck between the Christians and the Gypsies, who inhabited the quarter, immediately within the outer walls above the Albaizin.

All of this could have been avoided by the Moors if they had paid the tribute agreed upon ten years before in a deal with Ferdinand and Isabella. The Moorish ruler Boab-Dil had pledged a tribute payment in gold to the Spanish Sovereigns, and had failed to pay. He was in Default. So Catholic Isabella and her Ferdinand raised an army to lay siege and effect the "Reconquesta" which was supposed to be the final chapter in the entire re-Christianization of Spain. Or at least most of it. The Alhapurras and much of the southeastern corner of the country remained in Moorish hands until a revolt a hundred years ago was brutally put down and the last moors were forcibly relocated; Most have returned, to the isolated and defensible towns

The Gypsies had an important role in the fall of the Alhambra. The key element in ousting the Moors from the impregnable Alhambra was a deal struck between the Christians and the Calo's, who inhabited the quarter called the “Sacromonte”, immediately within the outer walls above the Albaizin. (Present day Arab Barrio)

The “Sacromonte” lies within the outer walls of the castle complex. Running along the top of the ridge behind the castle the besieging Christian armies had no way of breaching the walls. The rigged terrain prohibited getting siege engines into place so the Christian armies and knights were powerless to cut off supplies, and reinforcements coming in from up the mountain side.

The deal was offered by the Christian Monarchs. The Calo's were promised their freedom under Catholic rule, but they must embrace Christianity. The Calo's had privately practiced their own form or spiritual, musical, spirit calling and communication with ancestors at family gatherings for centuries, even thousands of years going back to Vedic times in the Indian Sub-continent. They had no problem assimilating the Christian ideas into their lives. The Calo's had survived six centuries of Moorish bondage by being adaptable. They saw no conflict in the belief systems. They embraced Catholicism, and kept their usual rituals private.

They told the the Spanish Rulers that their “duendes” (spirits) were just the lost souls of unbaptized babies.

Isabella loved that. It was rumored among the gypsies that she also liked Columbus but that’s another story.

The Calos made a hole in the outer wall from the inside out which can be seen to this day. The Christian knights were able to enter and fighting on a down hill slope through the Albaizin, from street to street, in furious conflict, they took the outer walls. This still left the steep cliffs up to the Alhambra which was still completely secure behind the inner walls. A city state fortress with an internal water supply and soaring totally impregnable defenses still intact.

The problem for Boab–Dil, was that with the outer walls invested with Christian troops, he could no longer be resupplied with food from the mountains above the castle. He was doomed to surrender or starve.

Negotiations between nobles were elaborate and complex. Technically the key issue was still the payment of the gold which Boab-Dil either didn't have or refused to pay. Now isolated and cut off, he had to accept being "evicted". The terms of the surrender were foolish for the Christian Kings. In return for the physical keys to all the gates and doors. Boab-Dil was allowed to leave with his baggage, troops, and retinue, was given a huge secure area in south eastern Spain for his people and granted terms of import and travel which was to prove troublesome, even ruinous to future generations of Spaniards.

The Famous "Reconquesta" wasn't quite what it seemed. Yes it was true that The Alhambra was the last strong point to fall back into Christian hands, but the terms of the surrender were actually quite favorable to the Moors, and left them with the southern slopes of the Alhapurras as their "fief" and the terms of the peace agreement gave the Moors free rights to come and go from the Spanish mainland for the purposes of "trade", Also the Alhapurras were as defensible in their own way as the Alhambra had been.

The Moors continued to be a problem in Spain for the next few hundred years. They would raid the lowlands from the mountain strongholds. And were impervious to counter measures, because of the incredibly rough terrain and narrow passes. The Alhapurras are the second highest mountains in Europe. The Christian Kings eventually fought there way up the mountains to the town of Lanjaron and established a chain of watch towers that could send fire signals from mountain top to mountain top enabling word of hostile and raiding landings on the coast to be flashed to Granada within minutes. The towns above Lanjaron remained in Moorish hands until a century ago and even today are hostile to Christian intruders.

The Sacromonte

In choosing Granada as my destination I was influence by the fact that despite its bad rep in the guide books, the Sacromonte (Sacred Mountain) was probably the oldest Gypsy neighborhood in Spain. The City of Granada had more luthiers then any other city its size, and there was a school, high above the city in the caves of the Sacromonte, called "Carmen of the Caves."

A little homework on the internet produced a list of the luthiers in the city of Granada and with a couple emails I was enrolled in some basic courses at the School.

Tickets for flights to Malaga were about $350.00 round trip at the time. Over the next several years I went through a couple dozen of them.

In many ways Flamenco has become a standardized, vulcanized, homogenized, certified standard issue export product. Within its ranks are most of the finest players, singers, and dancers in the world. Many of them totally unknown outside the private Spanish world of Flamenco Associations. It is this network of flamenco association that keep the art alive, rewards those who keep its traditions, and fosters and celebrates the artists and moments that reach back in time to tap into the spirit that inspires the great present day artists. The Calo's gather in extended family groups every weekend in caves, homes and halls to continue musical and spiritual traditions that were brought to Spain from Carnatic (southern) India 1200 years ago.

In the real world of Flamenco there are over 400 listed private Flamenco associations in Spain. They are all private. Closed to outsiders. No "Payos" (non-gypies) allowed unless brought by a member, who better have a good reason.

I arrived in the late winter of 2000 on a flight from NY to Malaga, brief stop in Madrid. It was the first trip since 63 and a short visit in the mid 70's when I had driven through the country from Bilbao to Madrid and out through Barcelona, stopping only to buy an inexpensive guitar from Jose Ramirez.

This time was different I was alone, solvent, and there to study. Driving to Granada from Malaga only took a few hours and I found my self parked below the Alhambra. Leaving the car, I spent hours on climbing on foot before finally finding the school high up on the hill on a street that was barely accessible by foot let alone cars. With great relief I found the place and a young fellow showed my to an apartment I had rented for my stay. Once behind multi-locked and barred doors I felt a little more comfortable leaving my things and went out to explore the neighborhood.

I had been there less then a couple hours and was walking towards the "Plaza Chico" a local square when a tattered Motorcycle pulled up. A young woman jumped off the rear seat and announced that she was a the 15th incarnation of Saint Katherine. She said that they had heard that I was there and the driver of the motorcycle was Cameron, who would be my teacher. The driver looked like the Muppet's drummer. You know, the one who had his shoes nailed the floor to keep him from chasing cars? I think his name was Animal. Over time I got to know this particular character from the first afternoon and he was in fact a totally dedicated flamenco singer who lived in poverty and sang the "bulerias"as his specialty. It was a great introduction to the culture.

Anyway, a word about Cameron De la Isla (pronounced Cameroon) who, in a sense, is the Calo Gypsy Elvis. Acclaimed by all in the gypsy world to be the greatest singer who ever lived Cameron died about ten years before. But not in spirit. His picture is on the wall over every bar in the Sacromonte and every Gypsy Flamenco Bar in Spain. In a world often filled with dissent there is no dissent over Cameron . He was the greatest, he still lives. Each weekend hundreds of remarkable lookalikes, go out for the weekends singing and dancing, dressed exactly like him, singing his songs, and saying I am not dead I was just hiding. Cameron was and is the defining artist in the Flamenco world. Paco de Lucia and Tomatito are the two greatest guitarist is Spain today and they both worked for years as Camaron's accompanist.

The next day I had an appointment in the afternoon with my teacher from the school and spent the morning visiting some of the 27 luthier shops, at the foot of the hill near the Plaza Grande.

I had worked my way up one of the streets leading to the Castle that had several luthier shops. I was meeting the guitar-makers and trying the various instruments. I was just entering the shop of Manuel Diaz, when I literally bumped into Mike Jingles.

I didn't know it then but it was to be a life changing encounter. Mike was carrying three guitars and was wearing a shirt made out of an American flag. He spoke Spanish with a British accent, and in fact was a Brit who had grown up in the local Gypsy culture. He was completely accepted by the Gypsies, and was a poplar member of the local scene. He spoke excellent Spanish, Calo, and was the most knowledgeable English speaking Guitarist and student of the culture with its obscure historical sources and subtle variations of all the basic themes that I had ever met before or since. He was an ongoing life student of the most obscure minutia of the art form and was a treasure trove of fact and information. He also was a friend of Paco de Lucia's, and taught the fingering and scale techniques that let the master players roam over the fretboard with such seeming effortless ease.

We hit it off immediately. He invited me up to his house in the Albaizin. And a few hours later I went. I had not been there a half hour and was looking through Mikes instrument collection when there was a knock at the gate. It was Emilio Maya, who was scheduled to be my teacher at the school. Small world, this Flamenco world. He and Mike were "scale exercise partners" a regime of practice routines to develop the hands.

We spent the afternoon talking, playing, smoking, and playing some more. Emilio and Mike were close friends and I began to realize what a small and tight knit community this was. I played for Emilio, and he was very impressed, and declared me to be "the best North American Guitarist he had ever heard". High praise coming from him, Like Mike says:"Emilio is a genuine Calo guitar Master, and was he was equally regarded as a singer." Most Calo Gypsies are singers. The music is based on the Sanscrit Ragas of India dating back more than three thousand years. It originally was a singing art form that developed over time into the standardized presentations of today.

Emilio was then and still is the top player in the Sacromonte. This is the same neighborhood that produced, Estrella Morentis (current absolute queen of the Spanish Pop and Flamenco world), and the great legendary Carman Amaya. There are others, like David Carmona, and many other players who remain unknown to the outside world, but who all can play rings around the best US players. Emilio had risen to the top the year before when the previous top player in the city Pepe Habichuela had moved on to the top rung of the Flamenco world, Madrid.

For the next several weeks I adapted to life in the neighborhood, learned my way around and, over time, visited the various venues. Finding the music was easy. You just had to walk and follow your ears. The guide books were all totally wrong. The Sacromonte neighborhood, with its stunning views of the Alhambra was perfectly safe. It was a good idea to stay out of the Arab neighborhood below called the Albaizin late at night, but only the lower part was dangerous, and that not much different then the lower east side of NY. The difference was that in the lower Albaizin there was a dark twisted labyrinth of narrow streets where non gypsies were not welcome.

I took lessons from Emilio, and Hung out with Mike Jingles. The gypsies had given Mike his name '"Jingles" because he always had a little cash on hand to buy and trade for instruments which he had restored by the luthiers in town and then sold to students or exported to England. Mike kept trying to explain to me what he said was this important theory, but I was resistant. At first I didn't really understand what he was talking about.

A few week later, toward the end of my first visit, I was coming up to my last weekend. Weekends are important in the Gypsy culture because it's when they get dressed up in what we would call their "Sunday best" and "go Flamenco" visiting all the caves and venues singing, sharing, dancing, and playing. For them it has spiritual significance and they take it very seriously.

There was a venue I had heard of that was called Pepe's. According to rumor it had been hosting a hard-core gathering in the same location for more than 400 years. It was in the lower Albaizin in the no-non-gypsies-allowed area and at the entrance to the neighborhood there was a sign painted on the wall, "beware, muggers, thieves". The rumor also was that if you went there and they didn't like your playing they would break your guitar and beat you or worse before throwing you out.

I decided to go, but I left my guitar at home, and invited another one of the students from the school with me. Pepe's was a venue in the oldest section of the Albaizin. He was only open on Saturday nights from midnight on until well past daybreak Sunday morning. We arrived a few minutes before 12 and Pepe was alone except for a kid about 14 in the corner fooling with a guitar. Pepe was behind behind the small bar washing glasses. I introduced myself as being from the School, and told him I was a student of Emilio's. He waved us to a seat near the door. Shortly later a rough looking man came in followed by the first few patrons.

The man ordered a drink at the bar and looked around. He saw me sitting quietly, and became visibly upset. He approached and began to speak. "People come here and think it is some kind of show" he said. He did something with his wrist and a long knife appeared in his hand. "They don't realize that they are not welcome. When that happens we cut them up a little and do a flamenco dance on their corpses out in the street." As he said that, as if by magic, another equally long and glittering knife appeared in his other hand.

Pepe called from behind the bar "It's OK, hes a student of Emilio's, wait, he'll play something for you." He nodded to the kid who was sitting in the corner, who had been fooling with an old guitar that belonged to the house. They handed the guitar to me

By then I had some experience with the "house guitars" of Gypsy caves, bars, and venues. They often were nearly unplayable, beyond battered with high actions, holes in the wood, and more often then not were used for rhythm, rather then lyrical playing. Pepes "house guitar" was much better than most in terms of condition and the height of the action, but when I tried to tune and play a chord in the first position I was dismayed to find no wrappings on the strings. They had been completely worn away in the first 4 positions. It was impossible to get a clean note. Pepe had come out from behind the bar and I now had a half dozen suspicious Gypsies, one of them armed, in a semi circle around my chair. The young student that I had brought with me was looking quite alarmed.

I looked up to Pepe, "Have you got a capo" I wanted to shorten the fretboard and maybe find some wrappings on the strings further up the neck. Pepe produced a capo. I tried the capo at the second fret, still no traction, third fret same thing. Finally with the capo in the fourth position there were wrappings (the fine wire that wraps around the nylon center threads of the strings), at the 4th fret. I tuned and made a disclaimer. I told them that I had studied in Valencia 40 years before, and could only play what I had learned then. I began a Soleares. The palpably hostile atmosphere dissipated immediately. The kid from the corner of the room who had been fooling with the guitar and had been salivating at the prospect of seeing the "payo" cut up and thrown out, looked as though he had been clubbed, his jaw fell open. The fellow with the knives made them disappear back into his sleeves. A smile spread across Pepe's face. When I finished there was dead quiet but they were all nodding encouragement. "what else can you play?" asked Pepe. One by one I played Soleares, Alegrias, Farruca, and Taranta. They loved it. Pepe said "he plays exactly like someone from 40 years ago".

It was a perfect moment. The guy with the knives bought me a drink, and so did Pepe. They didn't change the position of the capo or alter the tuning for the rest of the night. The place quickly became jam packed and the playing, dancing, singing and clapping went on till dawn and beyond. I finally left around 7 AM and could still hear the clapping as I walked up the steep narrow streets toward my place. Just before I left two things happened that put a perfect cap on the night. A women leaned over and spoke to me. "We can see by the light in your eyes that you truly love our music and our culture. We have been here for the last four hundred years, sharing the spirit that flows from here. You will always be welcome here to share the spirit" The other thing was from the guy who had the knives. We left at the same time and out in the street he shook my hand and told me I was a great player. Over the course of the evening he had been playing, singing, dancing and showing a lady friend his "girdle" of leather armor packed with gold coins tucked into separate slit pouches that protected his midriff in combat. About as hard core and classic as it get's. I felt honored by his compliment.

During this trip, I attended a show at a large Arab venue in the Albaizin. The form

“Zambras” was popular with the Arabs as was all Flamenco. I hadn't heard it since Montoya, and was thrilled to find it in its natural habitat. I was invited to play and did so. It went well, I got some traction and they liked my stuff. They invited me back for an evenings gig, shared with a lady Romany violinist about a week later. This was a part of the Flamenco world unknown to me before. The Violinist played classic style of the Roma, not the wild passionate frenzied playing of the movies, but simple folk and traditional melodies, played as though standing around a campfire. A friend of hers was a gypsy belly dancer who went through multiple costume changes and danced between pieces played by the violinist and myself. It was a very small gig really, but it was my first in Spain.

Anselma's, The Triana

I came back to Spain a few months later. This time I brought my friend Linda, and rented a house with a lovely view of the Alhambra from the Sacromonte (Gypsy neighborhood above Granada). We enjoyed the life and life style. There are always lots of concerts and activities in Granada especially in the Arab cafes. It was always interesting. We had come in on a flight from Madrid, so since we had a rental car we decided to check out some of the other Andalusian Cities that had a large concentrations of Flamenco. Notably Cordoba, Seville, and Moron de la Frontera.

We arrived in Seville, checked into a hotel and went looking around the Flamenco venues. The first night I couldn't sleep so I went out for a walk and wound up jamming at a sidewalk cafe with a large group of musicians who had just finished work and were rehearsing together, It was a great introduction to the spirit of the City.

Several of the venues were commercial tourist shows, but one was large, interesting, and genuine. "Anselma's" was a Flamenco bar venue in the Triana (gypsy barrio made famous in the opera "Carmen") that opened at 12 midnight and went until dawn four nights a week, Wednesday through Saturday.

We went in and sat down. I had my guitar case with me. It was crowded, there was no stage just an area by one wall underneath a Statue of the Patron Saint of the Gypsies. Anselma was the lead singer and in a way was sort a sort of a female Spanish Lord Buckley. There were over a hundred people there and she called them her "children" and was very very much in charge. The bar was busy and three deep, we were lucky to have a table on the edge of the band. One of the guitarist made eye contact to me and indicated my guitar case with a lifted eyebrow. His name was Fernando. He leaned over and asked me to play, so I opened the case and pulled out my guitar.

The band was just starting another number, there were three singers four or five rhythm guitars, a couple cojon (rhythm) players and constant guests. They played in a circle and the dancers and singers performed in the center of the circle. A young man laughed when I opened my case and pointed me out to his girl friend, "look he chortled, the Payo is going to play, this'll be good." He was grinning. The band began the piece and it was a Solea de Triana which is a "Soleares" that includes a G7th Chord. After a moments tuning I fit in and took off. I sort of lost control a little, I just tore into the piece with scales and passion. The piece ended and I got many nods of approval, The kid with the grin looked shocked.

The band started into the next piece. It took me a moment to realize that they were playing in G, but the moment I realized it I dropped the two bottom strings into a G tuning and took off again. This time I really went away. I was so caught up in the music and the moment, that I didn't realize that I had become the driving force of the piece or more accurately, that they were driving me. I was so engrossed, that I became oblivious to my surroundings. I didn't notice that the entire band had formed a circle around me and were totally jamming. It was another great moment. We finished the piece and the place cheered.

From then on I had a permanent seat in Anselma's Band. She introduced me to the audience, and said they didn't know my name but had decided to call me Jhonny. It was a few years later that I asked someone why she called me Johnny. I was told, "Jhonny Guitar" of course. Anselma told the people of the Triana that I was proof that Gypsy souls come back in the bodies of "others". It was also proof that "Anselmas" wasn't a bar, or a nightclub, or a venue, but a church! "how do we know it's a church?" she asked. "Because miracles happen here. Here is a man who speaks very little Spanish, and almost no gypsy at all and yet he plays with hands of silver. Only god can do that". It was the first of what was to become many wonderful evenings.

The next trip I brought two of my adult sons. I rented the same house above the caves of the Sacromonte, and rented an adjoining apartment which we set up as a classroom so that one of the local Calo Gypsy teachers could teach my sons basic Flamenco. My theory was that it would be a fresh approach for them, and they would absorb it quickly.

At the end of a week we went to a local restaurant for dinner, it was the same place that I had played on my first trip. At the end of dinner the boys went to pay the check. They were told that there money was no good there. They said "what do you mean, why not?" The answer was "because your with him" indicating me. Its not easy to impress your kids these days, but that was a great moment for me. The boys were really amazed.

The next day we left for Seville in the early evening arriving there in the wee hours. Checking into a pension, we went looking for an open restaurant and came upon the one where I had jammed with the band on a previous trip. As we ate our sandwiches and tapas, one by one the musicians from the same band arose and stopped by the table to greet and shake my hand. The boys were impressed again. "gee Dad, do you know every musician in Spain?" I explained that I had jammed with them before on my first night on a earlier trip. The boys and I hung out at Anselma's, attended the "Festival at

Jerez" and got to hear and see many of the greatest players, singers, and dancers, in the genre.

Jerez de la Frontera, was historically one of the most prosperous cities in Andalucia, through trade in Sherry and its close proximity to the ports of Seville and Cadiz.
The wealthy Sherry Houses sponsor a Flamenco Festival each year which brings the best talent and greatest artists. Some are obscure, but all are the best in the world.

After several performances in succession one of my sons told me "if you had told me two weeks ago that I would watch an opera four nights in a row and looking forward to a fifth I would have said you were nuts."

Bringing my sons to Spain and teaching them about the gypsy culture did not go unnoticed. The Calo's of the Sacromonte observed and approved.

For the next few years I would play at Anselma's whenever I was in Spain which was 2 or three times a year. Arriving at Malaga on a Wednesday morning I would drive to Seville, stay in a pension next to the gig and play four night from Wed to Sat. Then I would typically leave for the Costa del Sol and my haunts in the Sacromonte above Granada. Mike Jingles was living in a house on the coast in Almunecar, about an hours drive from Granada. Early in the week I would hang with Mike "Jingles" and his friends and he would inundate me with scale charts, triads, and fretboard theory. Mike had a young Russian genius classical player studying with him, that could think in difficult musical dimensions. Even Mike was very impressed.

Mike was proud of his friend ship with Paco De Lucia, and Paco would occasionally call. Mike was always fascinated by what new challenges Paco would invent for himself. And would say "If you don't think that Paco de Lucia is the greatest guitarist in the work then listen again". Rumors flew in the flamenco world about what "Paco" was up to along with "Tomatito" and "Moraito" who are two more legendary players in Spain. Vincente Amigo is a recent Superstar, and every few years another phenomenal player emerges.

Mike insisted on my grasping a fundamental concept that he kept trying to explain to me."You play fine Peter, but you have to learn this in order to be free". I just didn't get it yet, but I paid attention, took notes, wrote out scales and fingerings on fretboard charts, and tried to figure out what he meant.

The Trial

On another trip I was playing in the rear cave at Antonio Carmona (senior)'s "Cueva Bulerias, when a formal complaint was made about the "Conde Hermanos" guitar I was playing. It was a guitar that Mike Jingles had bought cheaply from an Italian Gypsy and had extensively and expensively restored before selling it to me. It had a new fretboard, new frets, and many major repairs, but the former owner recognized it's sweet sound and was devastated. The complaint that he made was a demand for a trial. It was a Gypsy custom. He argued that the instrument was a cultural treasure, and had been played by Cameron, Tomatito, and Paco de Lucia and many others. It should not leave the Sacromonte. This was serious, the doors were blocked.

There was a guest in the front cave that was a world class singer. The Gypsies were diplomatic and made their case. They explained that this was a formal complaint and trial. "Now we will show you" said the singer. And he sang while someone else played my guitar. It sounded great of course. "You see? said the singer. "Now you play" he said. The beauty of the moment was that the other player took up the house guitar and played the "Palo" leaving me to trade lyrical lines with singer. It was great, we flew together around the interior of that cave like Jonathan Livingston Seagull and his wing-man. I had been practicing in the key he was singing in and it worked perfectly, like a spiritual miracle. They yelled Ole, and wished me well with my guitar which I had earned the right to keep. The fellow who complained had to accept their verdict.

I continued to study with Mike in Almunecar, On the Cost del Sol. He often had a half dozen students and friends sleeping on the floor. I would ask him to show me things, like a proper introduction for a particular form, but he would say, "you are not ready yet". He would always return to the paper copies of the fretboard. "you have to see this in your mind" he said. "you can't look at the fretboard and decide which note to play, then tell the brain to send a message to the fingers to actuate the note, It takes too long! You have to see the notes in you mind and play directly from your mind to the instrument, not go back and forth." Like my childhood piano teacher he would then begin again at the beginning and lay out charts and scales, explain the intervals, major and minor and encourage me to write out the modes and scales on the paper copies of the fretboard. "To be able to write them on paper," he said, "is proof that you can see them in your imagination."

He said there was a pattern. I was still looking for it. I hadn't seen it yet.

I had taken some lessons from Emilio Maya but we had a falling out over a guitar purchase. I was walking in the upper Sacromonte one day when I noticed a small faded sign beside an old gate. It said, “Flamenco School”. The place looked very old and abandoned. There was a gate but it was chained shut and behind one could see an uneven patio with an old table and an assortment of odd chairs. Behind against the hillside was the entrance to an obvious ancient cave dwelling of unknown depth and complexity. There was a bell pull so I tried it, no response. I waited, then tried it again, then waited. After a long pause. the cave door opened. A man walked out. Each step he took was with a sweeping motion of his foot. He walked like a martial arts combatant entering the ring. He stared at me for what seemed like a long moment “What do you want?” he said. I told him that I was a player from NY, who wanted to learn to play for singers.

He said “come back tomorrow at four PM”. I did and he had me play for him. He accepted me as a student. This was my introduction to Antonio Maya. We became friends. Antonio's story was quite tragic. Many years before he had been coming home from the “Plaza Chico”. Most of the streets of the Sacromonte and Albaizin are as wide as your outstretched arms, too narrow for a car. Antonio was attacked with the intention of robbery by two men from Barcelona. Antonio is a classic Gypsy and so he fought back with his enormous folding knife. One of the assailants was killed. Antonio went to Prison. While he was in Jail he had to defend him self on several occasions. Other men died. Now, after years in prison, Antonio was reclusive, wary, and one of the finest people I have ever met. I am very lucky to have him as a friend and teacher. Because he is a Maya, he knows everyone in the Flamenco world but prefers to avoid crowds.

I was playing in Antonio's cave one night when a friend of his was over. I could hear them talking while I was playing. The friend said ”he's playing the singers part!” Antonio said “shhhhh he doesn't know he's doing it, isn't it great?” Antonio liked my playing and was eager to show me off to the other gypsies in his circle. He became my advocate. It was and is a good friendship. I am looking forward to going back now that I am much more fluent in Spanish.

After a couple years I read about a “Worlds Fair of Flamenco” that was going to be held in Seville. That turned out to be really significant. The fair itself drew all the talent from all over the country. It was a chance to see all the players, amateur and professional in the country. Also got a chance to play for and be heard by a lot of the players, singers, and members of the Flamenco community. There were jams at the instrument vendors, The booths representing the flamenco associational of nearly all the cities of Andalusia, in the stairs, doorways and hallways. It was perfectly acceptable to just open your case and play, and I did. Multiple theater venues had constant concerts and all the flamenco associations were represented, and competed to present their view of what flamenco was and who, in their view had been the most significant players.

Different cities competed vigorously to show that the origin of really great flamenco was from their city or area, and had elaborate chapter, verse and lineage to prove it. They each produced a series of concerts with the greatest singers, dancers and guitarists of their area. It was all fascinating.

It was a unique opportunity to gain an overview of the entire Flamenco world, but not quite all. Missing were the Romany violin lady, the Gypsy with the knives and girdle packed with gold coins. The wild Cameron look-a-like motorcyclist. The real flamenco of a real Saturday night in the poorer neighborhoods of Calo culture. All of these and quite a few others rejected association with such ”commercialization” on spiritual grounds.

But still it was a perfect view of the commercial side of the world of amateur and professional Flamenco. The winners of the local competitions from all over the country performed, and young fusion players and bands all appeared. Of Course all the great dance and performance companies of Spain presented their ballets, and spectaculars. The Seville Convention Center is huge with 5 theaters, and smaller performance spaces where artists gave workshops and talks. One had to prioritize, and maintain a tight schedule to take in as much as possible.

The first year I was just another tourist. I paid for my entry to the “Worlds Fair” and stayed at a hostal two doors from Anselma's in the Triana.

The best thing of all was that when the “Worlds Fair of Flamenco” shut down for the night around 12 PM Many of the players, bigwigs, and hard core people would head for Anselma's across the river in the Triana. I would be there playing in the band, and had a chance to be heard by everybody.

Over the three years that the Fairs were held, I moved up a small notch in status each year and became a more familiar figure. The second year I had professional credentials and passes to all the performances. The third year I had VIP passes and a free four star Hotel across from the Convention Center.

In the Sacromonte in Granada I regularly played in Antonio Carmona's “Cueva Bulerias”. When In Seville I played at Anselma's in the Triana, and during the week, studied with Mike in Almunecar on the Costa del Sol.

One day at the 3rd Worlds Fair I was walking from one event to another. A fellow began walking beside me. “I'm Jose” he said. ”That's great, hi Jose” I said. “Pepe sent me” he said. I didn't quite understand what he wanted, but he explained that people in the Sacromonte had been impressed with a jam session I had played in the Sacromonte a year before with Pepe. I clearly remembered it. It had been a great night and had been the first time that I played for Pepe while he was singing. Apparently it had apparently been memorable to more than just me. Jose said that people were still talking about “that night” “That's why Pepe sent me, he can't be here because he's singing in another city.I'm going to introduce you around”

Which he did. I met and played that afternoon for the delegation from two of the most prestigious competitions in the Flamenco world. This was a big deal for me. To win a competition in Spain in any one of the several important categories, was to insure that you would be fully employed at handsome rates for at least a year working just the 400 Flamenco associations who always booked the winners of the major competitions. It was serious money, and great glory.

The truth was that I wasn't ready yet. But I did have a breakthrough. Back in Woodstock on the large floor of my loft I laid out lines of papers, each page was a fretboard chart with a scale written on it. All of the scales of all of the modes of all of the keys. I was lining them up in rows looking for the “Pattern” that Mike had been talking about for the last four years. In moving the rows of scales, modes, and keys, I noticed that some of the same scales were used in other keys in other modes. I began to lined the rows up, moved them around, and walked around them trying to understand.

It hit me like an electrical shock, I had to be sure, I kept rearranging the rows and the pattern became obvious, finally. 65 years old and I finally understood something I should have learned 5O years earlier.

I called mike on his European cell phone. He was about to go on stage in Amsterdam where he was doing a seminar teaching this very subject. I said “Mike, it's CBAGFED isn't it! (referring to the never changing sequence of scale patterns that opened the doors to fretboard mastery.) “Ahhhhh, grasshopper,” he said, “come over and take the exam.”

I did, I flew over and took the same paper exam that I had flunked four years in a row. It was easy, once I understood. Mike would call out a key and a mode, and I would instantly write it out on a fretboard diagram. “What do I do now?” I asked Mike.

Jaleador – Spirit Caller

The adventures continued and began to flow together into a tapestry of spiritual moments. In the Triana one night my friend Fernando from Anselma's band was shouting in my ear while I played a long, long, long run in perfect compas for a packed house. “Now! Johnny Now! There are many great guitarists in the world but in this moment in time it is you who are the greatest, Now! Go! Johnny Go!”. The crowd went nuts. With this kind of environment and encouragement I played, as Anselma put it, “Sin Control” (out of control). But they liked it and word passed quickly when I was in town.

The lead male singer was unhappy that I would step on his lines occasionally, but after all I was playing the singers part too. One night I forgot to share the applause with traditional hand gestures after a standing ovation for a solo during one of his songs. I was moved back a row in the band for a week. I will be more careful in the future.

Back in the Sacromonte there was an all night Gypsy Disco on the main street of the neighborhood, which has a staggering view of the Alhambra on one side, and Gypsy caves, venues, houses, bars, and a terraced neighborhood up the mountainside on the left. The Gypsy disco is four stories tall, large, and was 5 Euros to enter, When the the city of Granada and it's 60,000 students closed down each evening around Midnight the bold and adventurous would come up the mountainside to the Sacromonte to drink until dawn and watch the sun come up from the top floor of the Disco.

My sons were on another floor, and I was sitting on a couch with my guitar. Over time, from complete immersion, my Spanish had improved dramatically. A young Gypsy woman who had obviously been drinking appeared with a tall tough character on either side. She said in Spanish “I can't fucking believe it! Right here in our own club! Goddam fucking YANKEES!” Payo meant non gypsy, Gringo meant foreigner, Yankee meant American equals imperialist bad guy. This was after 9/11 and after years of putting up with Basque separatist bombings the local community was outraged over our invasion of Iraq, bombing, etc etc.

I knew my usual “lo ciento no hablo ingles” (I'm sorry I don't speak English) wasn't going to do for this situation. “no Yankees (imperialists) here” I said. “Oh yehhh?”, she said, “whats your NAME!?” I said “Paco Pedro” (my Mexican nickname). She said “I've heard a lot of bullshit but that's the biggest load ever. PLAY me something PACO!” I said “sure, what would you like to hear, Soleares,? Alegrias,? Farruca? Guajiras?” She spat out the words “Give me a Bulerias!” Bulerias is not my strong suit, yet, but is one of my ambitions. I play the very basic stuff for dance classes occasionally here in the US so I started to play. Just the most basic form. The girl began to twirl and dance and snap her fingers over her head, as she danced away singing “Ole, Paco Pedro, Ole.”

The sessions down at the Cueva Bulerias had became a regular event. They usually would begin with just playing, then a singer or other guitarist would come in, then a couple more singers, then other people to clap the Palo, then more singers, and when the energy was hot the dancers would step into the center of the circle and explode with passionate energy. There were so many wonderful nights. One especially great one was with Pepe.

It was not long after that on the next trip, when I was carrying my guitar and walking down toward the Cueva Bulerias from my rental house three terraces above the main Street which was wide enough for cars and a small bus. As I walk down the steep cobbled street descending with a couple blocks to go I saw a large group of sinister appearing local young men in their teens to late twenties hanging out just ahead of me. There was about a dozen of them lounging on both sides of the street just past the corner. I could just as easily turn and descended by another route at the corner, but because they appeared to be the usual guys from the neighborhood, and because I knew the neighborhood knew of my tall strong sons, I decided to go straight through. It was the shortest way.

As I passed through the pack I said “buenas” they said “buenas” back. As I continued on down I could hear behind me one of the younger ones asking “who's he?” One of the older guys answered “oh him, he's the “Jaleador”. “Whats that?” said the younger one. The older fellow answered “He's the spirit caller, he's going down to Antonio's to call the spirits. We should go later, it should be a great session”.

“Hmmmm” I thought, “Jaleador,whats that about?” I asked Mike Jingles. “Ahhh” he said “Every Gypsy family has one person who keeps the faith and stays in touch with the spirits so he can call them for the family gatherings.” That person is called “The Jaleador” It means “Spirit Caller”

Too cool. I thanked God for my decision to return to Spain and resume the journey I had begun so many years before. I had found myself or at least had found my path.

Saint Sara

On one of the later journeys after the third "Worlds Fair" of Flamenco in Seville I was with my friend Linda and we were headed for Carmague France for the famous Gypsy festival of "Black Saint Sarah". After a night on the Costa del Sol, and a visit to Mike in Almunecar, we drove Murcia and visited the flamenco Association of the "Melon de Oro" (Melon of Gold). I had met them through Pepe's friend Jose at the last "Worlds Fair". They had invited me to come and play. It was one of the 3 top competitions in Spain, and I was eager to cultivate the contact. They were wonderful, warm cordial, welcoming and encouraging. It really was a preliminary trip for the following years festival and competition I was interested in learning how to enter and what was required, and about the categories and requirements.

We drove north, (it's a longish drive) to and through Barcelona and passing up through Girona and Catalonia we crossed the French Border and headed for the mouth of the Rhone River.

The Gypsy festival at Carmague (Saint Marie del Mar, France) is held the third week of May every year. The town is completely overrun by many thousands of Romany Gypsies and a few Calos. There is an apparent atmosphere of truce in regard to hostilities feuds, crime etc, and considering the many thousands in such a small space it is actually very peaceful and reverent.

This is a very serious religious tradition here, perhaps the most serious of all, dating back to 40 AD. The French police are VERY nervous. Not surprising when at least 20 thousand swarthy van living huge family groups amounting to many thousands of transients arrive in tiny San Marie del Mar to spend a week. They camp out everywhere in campgrounds that are traditional and ancient, and by the side of every road. The annual muggers and knife vendors convention is held the same week, jusst kidding ;) well almost. It is a good idea to be very polite and definitely don't hit on their woman, or even stare to long. It's also mating season and the huge annual social event brings out the provocative side of many of the young people.

There are music and dancing circles on every corner all week long and World class bands. Good food too. After "proving myself" by playing for a visiting Calo Singer I was excepted and had fun at several of the more intense sessions, just playing lead lines behind the singers. They gave me yet another Gypsy name, "El Piano" because they thought my playing sounded like piano playing.

With TV cameras in helicopters filming, and the thousands witnessing on the beach the Gypsy's reenact the rescue of Mary Magdalene from a dis-masted boat which allegedly included "the three Mary's" Mary Jacobi, Mary Salome, and Mary Magdalene in company with Lazarus and a young dark skinned girl who became know as Saint Sara and was alleged to be either:

A. An Egyptian Nun,

B: A servant of Mary Magdalene's,

C. The daughter of Jesus.

The bones have been carbon dated. They are from the first century. The boat came from Palestine. The story checks out to the extent possible. In any event thousands upon thousands of Gypsies flood the town, playing exotic "Jhango Reinhardt like Jazz" and singing like the Gypsy Kings. They all swear they have ancestors who were there at the time and that the stories are true.

The intriguing part is that it lends credence to the theory of "The Holy Grail" being the bloodline of Jesus, and rekindles and reinforces the ideas put forward in the "Davinci Code"

Pepe's Cave

After the Carmague trip I continued the series of what became routine journeys. Three or four times a year. Arriving at Malaga, then 4 days at Seville, then the early part of the week on the coast studying with Mike Jingles, and the second weekend in the Sacromonte playing in the caves. Toward the end of this series of trips, spanning a few years, I called Jose, and hooked up with Pepe.

Pepe wanted me to play for him in a competition. I was thrilled and honored. The problem was that I couldn't really give him what he wanted in terms of accompaniment. Not for a major national competition. I had almost no solo experience. Playing with a band had had given me many opportunities to solo, and quite a few standing ovations in Seville but I had very little real experience in the forms as a solo accompanist to a singer. I already had entered an important Competition in the guitarist category at a major festival one year, and although I was a clear crowd favorite, the judges disqualified me because I ran overtime. There was that time at the "Gypsy Trial for the guitar" but even then someone else was counting the palo on the house guitar. I could do it but just barely.

It was to be the most wonderful night of all in the Sacromonte. Pepe invited me to an evening at the "Plateria" The largest Private Flamenco Venue in Granada.

The Plateria is near the top of the Albaizin, and dates back hundreds of years, It is a walled compound maybe half a city block in size, and is located on the ancient "street of the guitar players" Inside there is a luxury restaurant, with hotel - like quarters above with charming balconies. and a huge out door seating area. There is also a respectable private theater. In appearance it resembles an upscale country club. It is totally closed to outsiders, with a security guard at the gate. Members only.

The members have their bills deducted from their bank accounts, and there are upstairs rooms in case one is too drunk to go home, or has formed a liaison with one of the pretty young gypsy girls, which abound within the closed society of the associations and which Pepe (who was in his seventies) was quite fond of. The place was called the Plateria, because each time a truly great Flamenco Artist passed on, a plate with their name on it was dedicated by the Board of directors and was hung on the wall. Hence Plateria. Pepe had already been awarded his plate. The only living person to enjoy that honor. At the end of the evening, after much drinking, many introductions, and attending a private concert in the theater, we retired to Pepe's venue/home/cave/bar/Flamenco Association and there amid the hundreds of awards, plaques, and statues that he and his family had won over the years at flamenco competitions along with a couple other guitarists and a bevy of young gypsy girls for clapping and shouting encouragement, we tried to work out some material together.

This was a real turning point. Despite my successes in Anselma's band in Seville, The magic nights in the caves, Mikes, Antonio's, and Emilio's training, I still didn't have the instinctive sure knowledge of the song structures, and the traditional phraseology of the accompanist. There was a fellow there who did this perfectly and it soon became apparent that I couldn't "Lead the piece" and "set the musical stage for the singer" I kept playing the singers part. I didn't have the discipline. They all agreed that the music I played was very beautiful, but it was not Flamenco in the traditional sense. They patiently explained that I needed to learn more about traditional accompaniment, and if I was going to go further, I needed to work on this skill. The good news was that after much discussion, and consultation, a firm consensus was reached that although my music wasn't exactly "Flamenco" it was very definitely very beautiful music. I would always be welcome.

Mike Jingles had taught me where all the notes were in any mode or key, Antonio had showed me who the great artists were and why they were the greatest. I now had the basic skills required, but it was now necessary to return to square one and learn the skill and art of traditional accompaniment. I'm told it's not hard, I have all the necessary skills, but need to study the traditional song structures, learn some songs, not Flamenco forms but songs. I only recently started translating songs, and the subtle variations appear to be endless. It will take time, more time for me because I grew up counting in threes and fours, played diatonic and minor scales and chords, and played songs that were based on a standard western verse chorus formula.

On one of my first trips while playing in the "Cueva Bulerias" one evening I could hear two people behind me talking. One said "ask him, go ahead and ask him. Ask him for a capo". No I don't want to" said the other voice "no, go ahead ask him" said the first voice. I felt a tap on my shoulder, "Have you got a capo?" I fished around in my shirt pocket and handed him a block, string and peg traditional capo. "See said the first voice, I told you, he likes the old ways". The second voice said "yes and he plays very well but I noticed that he doesn't play much in the key of E." With a trace of sadness in his voice the first voice said noooo, no he doesn't". "Why do you think that is" said the second voice?". The first voice answered "ohhh bad upringing I guess. It's the parents fault"

For the next three weeks wherever I went people would say "Pedro look at this" and show me things in the key of E. It was taking the whole village to educate the child.

I was perfectly willing to learn traditional accompaniment and had lined up a teacher to work with me on this, when there came a knock on my door just as I was packing for another trip. It was Josh Rosenthal from Thompkins Square Fantana/Universal Record Company. He wanted me to record some raga pieces for a tribute album. Josh told me that I had influenced other players and he had organized a tribute album called "A Raga For Peter Walker".

Here and Now

It became a complete change of direction, I opened up the case on the steel string, recorded what he wanted, and for the next few years toured in the US and Europe in support on what became four record releases. “A Raga For Peter Walker”, “Echo of My Soul”, “Spanish Guitar”, and “The Long Lost Tapes”. My current Release is “Has Anybody Seen Our Freedoms”.

Years ago in Franco's Spain in early 1964 after coming out of north Africa I used to sit in cafes in Algeciras, and listen to Flamenco on the jukebox, and watch the traditional evening promenade of the young ladies going one way and the young men going the other way around the town square. That same month I heard the passionate, spontaneous“Saeta” during Holy week. To experience these moments is to enrich your soul. Spain and the Gypsy culture are changing fast. It is harder and harder to find authentic examples. Follow your ears in the Sacromonte, and you will find it if that's what you are seeking.

Over the last 14 years I have had a chance to renew my education in Spain, with great teachers, and much acclaim. I hope to record more, and take snapshots of my growth like litmus paper in the chemical brew of life. I am 75, and life gets more exciting every day. Living in the Latin culture, learning the ancient theory's of the guitar. I feel uniquely blessed to have achieved many of my goals. Life has exceeded my expectations.

Albert Grossman (who managed Dylan and PPM) said something to me once that Maynard Solomon instinctively had been aware of back in the Vanguard days of the 60's. He was explaining to me why he came to my obscure little local Woodstock gigs. He said “The common denominator of music that achieves greatness, is that it carries the listener away, takes them out of themselves for an interlude somewhere else, somewhere beautiful, or poignant, and then brings them back. You always do this in least once in every performance, but just for a few moments, if only you could do it consistently”. Coming from him, it was the best complement and greatest encouragement I ever had, Since then I have tried to acquire the skills and tools to achieve that goal, I hope that I have succeeded.

In 2008, I was listening to a program one night on a solitary drive from Madrid to

Barcelona. The leg of the tour had included four cities in Catalonia, four in Portugal and wound up with a concert on the last night in Madrid. The show was in a Gypsy Venue, and as one writer later wrote, It was a special challenge for a non gypsy to play there. What if they didn't like it?

The gig had gone great I love the gypsy community. They are such loving people to each other, (except for occasional feuds). I had been playing at a venue frequented by many gypsies from the "Worlds Fairs of Flamenco" that had been held in Seville for three years and word travels fast in the Gypsy world. Also they had been told about some of my teachers. Rumor was that I was a gringo who was living proof that gypsy souls inhabited other bodies so they were willing and eager to listen.

I screwed up the first two pieces. Missed a couple notes with the left hand and missed a couple plucks with the right hand. It is legal to smoke in Madrid. So I stopped, stepped to the rear of the stage, and took a toke. Then I got traction and went into my concert presentation, with a couple exotic forms, and tunings, they loved it. It was a great gig and went on generating more and more energy. I played all my stuff. It took an hour and a half, the large dark basement venue was thick with smoke and crammed with people applauding and cheering. I said "that's all I've got, that's it". There was a quick buzz and they hollered back "Play The First Two Again.!" I did and they were flawless. It took everything up to another level. It was perhaps the best gig of my life. (Got a good review too).

Anyway, I had to return the rental car in Barcelona and take a flight in the morning, so I left Madrid navigating by compass toward the northeast highway and a short time later I was driving through the moonlit night, coasting on the high from the gig, and making the 6 hour journey in complete solitude with Spanish National Radio in the Car. I was lucky, that at this time, at a high point in my playing life, that I should listen to several hours of some of the best music ever played. It was all guitar music. It was great, it was precise and clean, perfectly articulated.. It showed me how far I have yet to go. The program was a collection of string works over several centuries and the thing they all had in common was the precise and beautiful intonation of the music ideas, and the uncanny ability to transport the listener to celestial realms.

I wrote to a friend in Catalonia, "My guitar is my voice, the notes are my words"

Ali Akbar Khan (Khan Sahib) says: "Music is not for wealth, fame, or even the pleasures of the mind, but is for true spiritual advancement. This I truly believe".

Timothy Leary said: "He plays on the ancient protean strings of the genetic code"

Genetic codes and memories are things that can be tapped into. I'm singing my ancestors songs through my instrument, and in the Gypsy culture, they get it. I love it.

Appendices

General info;

The guitar in the story of the “Gypsy Trial” was/is a Conde Hemanos 1970

Finger nails short. On right hand - just past the edge of the pad of the fingers.

Don't practice mistakes, practice perfection.

Music is a language that talks about feelings.

When practicing basic scales in the first position treat the nut like it was a fret and articulate the scales without using the index finger of the left hand,or better yet, “fret the nut”. Play the nut with the index finger as though it was a fret. This is to develop the left hand.

If you are going to Spain to study it is a basic courtesy to learn the language, and it will really speed up the learning process. Making lists of words and phrases on flash cards and reviewing them over breakfast was a big help. Lately I have gone months at a time immersed in the Peruvian culture not speaking English and read and write the language every day. Like music, try to develop an ear for the different accents.

Flamenco was/is a singing art form long before the guitar was developed. If you can sing it, or if you can dance it, you can play it.

Tuning: Realize that the equal–tempered tuning is full of compromises, and don't be afraid to tweak your tuning to the key you are playing in. Make sure it sounds balanced in the first, fifth and 10th position. Drop the 6th string to D to play in D, leave the 6th string in D and lower the 5th string one tone to G to play in G. both of these result in easier fingerings on the top four strings.

My own favorite albums are: Rainy Day Raga, Spanish Guitar, Raga for PW, and Freedoms. A couple of the cuts from 2'nd poem are really nice.

My current concert instrument is a Manuel Diaz from Granada. The wood is from the Alhambra, and is 1200 years old. The personal dedication inside tells the history of the wood and the sentiments of the maker. He writes that the making of a modern guitar out of the ancient wood produces “A new guitar with an old soul.” It has a name inscribed. It is called “The Legend of Andalusia”. It is a perfect replica of the 1864 Torres Guitar that was the first modern Guitar, ever. Senor Diaz built four of them. I am privileged to own one of them. I play it in every key every day.

I play the Raga's on a six string steel Gibson Dreadnaught. Light gauge bronze strings.

The CD “Spanish Guitar” was recorded on the Conde Hermanos.

I will record more, some songs, and especially compositions on Spanish Guitar.

LEVEL 1

APPENDIX 1: Palmer French Music theory, Basic Chords

When you look at the patterns made by a single vibrating string in the diagram below you can see that there are key points in the cycle of the vibrating string. It is the coincidence of these frequencies which is the basis of Harmony.

A "perfect octave" is the most perfect mathematical harmony and sounds perfect to the human ear. The 5th interval of the 7 note scale sounds harmonious but slightly less so. So does the 4th. All Chords are based on the "Triad" of the first third and notes from the root tone. Fun stuff. Take a string, a long one, pluck it, watch the patterns, when you are playing, try and put your next note in the exact middle of the pattern that you made with the first note.

The following 2 pages contain the basic chords for playing in all the basic major keys, and the two most common Phrygian Modal keys.

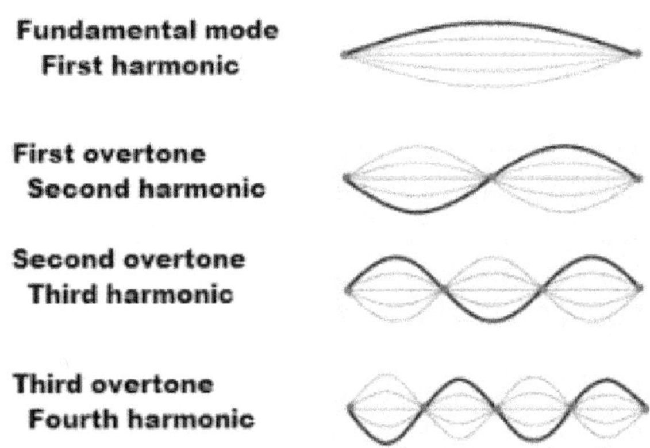

Fig. 1

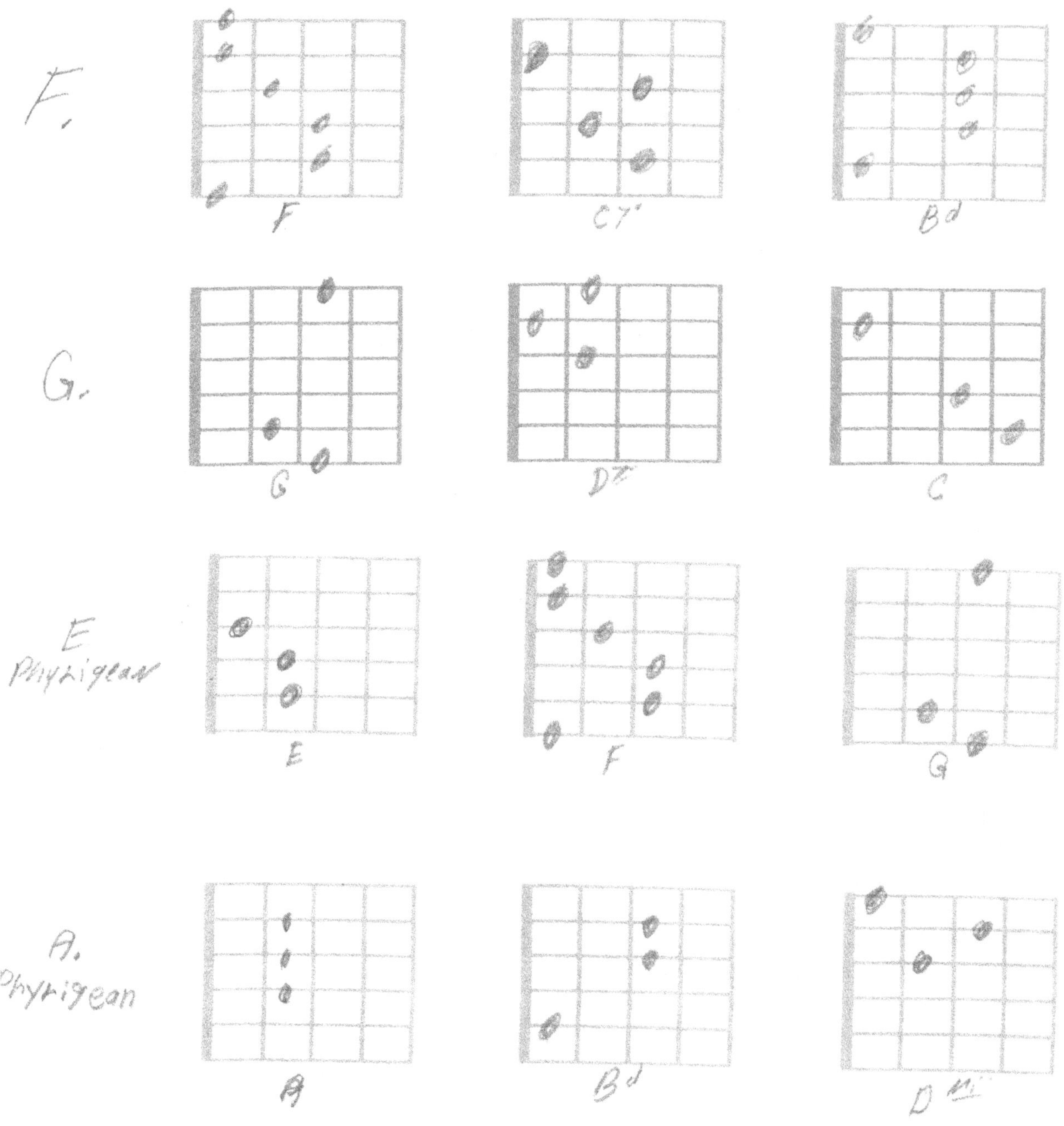

The basic chords can be found in 6 places up the fretboard using the keyword CAGED

CAGED is a system for transposing chords up the neck
If you place your index finger across the neck at the top
of the previous chord and fret the next chord in sequence

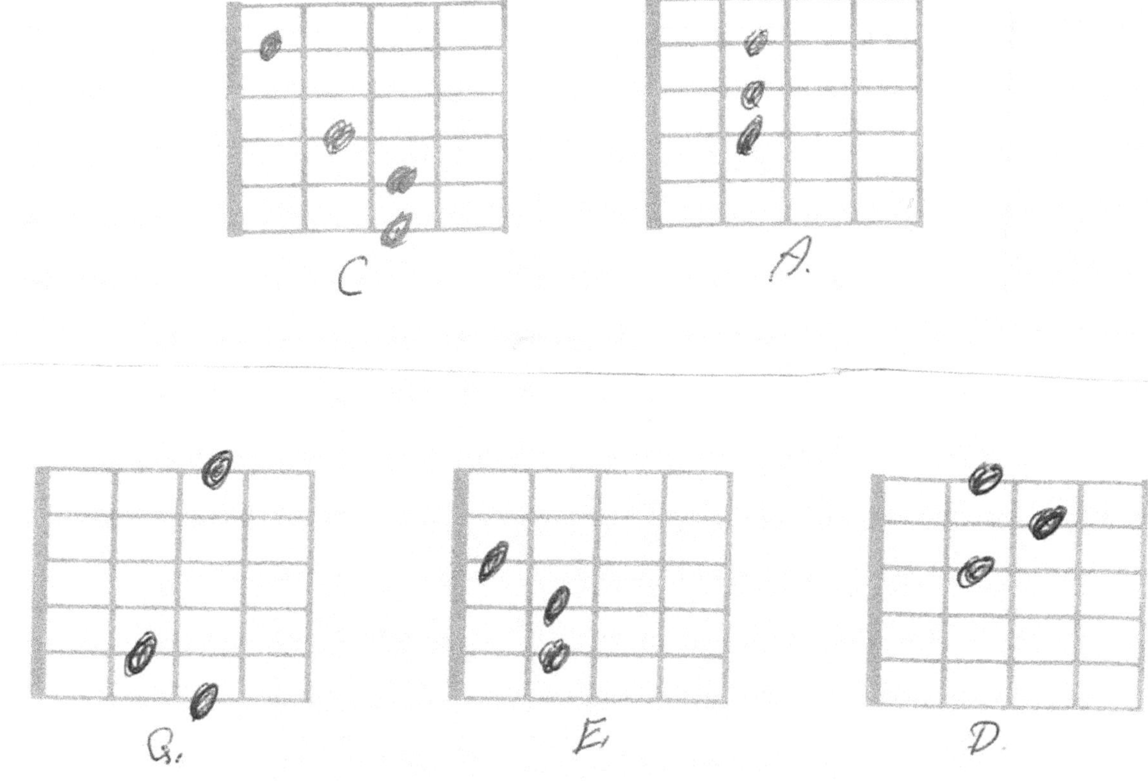

you will easily find the next fingering for the same chord.

These 5 chord formations repeat up the neck to produce the same chord. Here is an example of the five C chords available to you going up the neck using the CAGED system. The point is that the Pattern will never change, up and down, and you will always be able to find all the inversions of the basic chords.

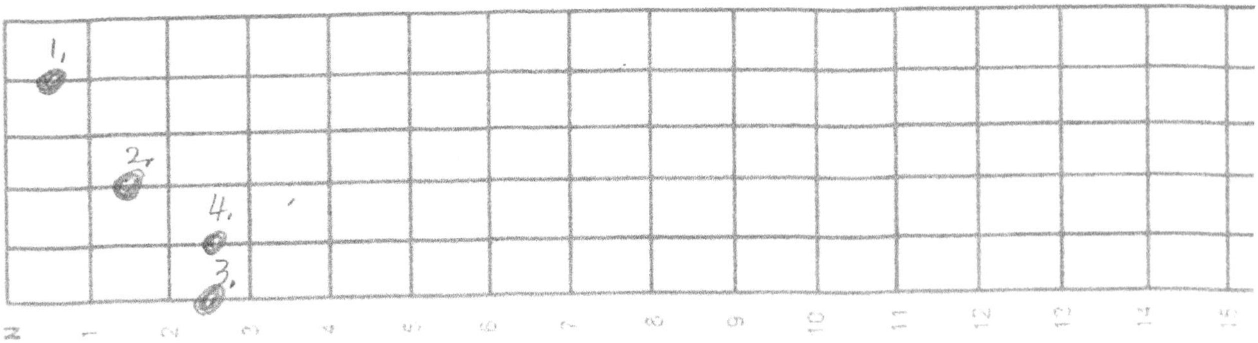

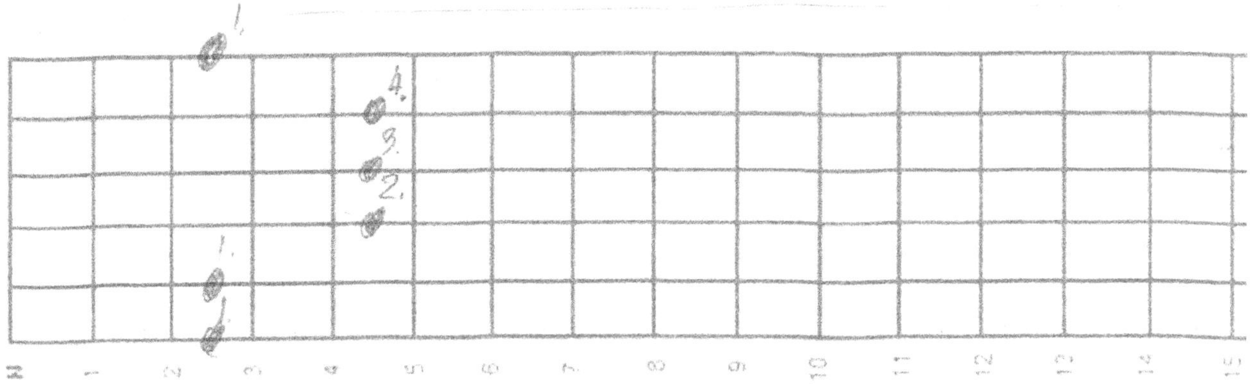

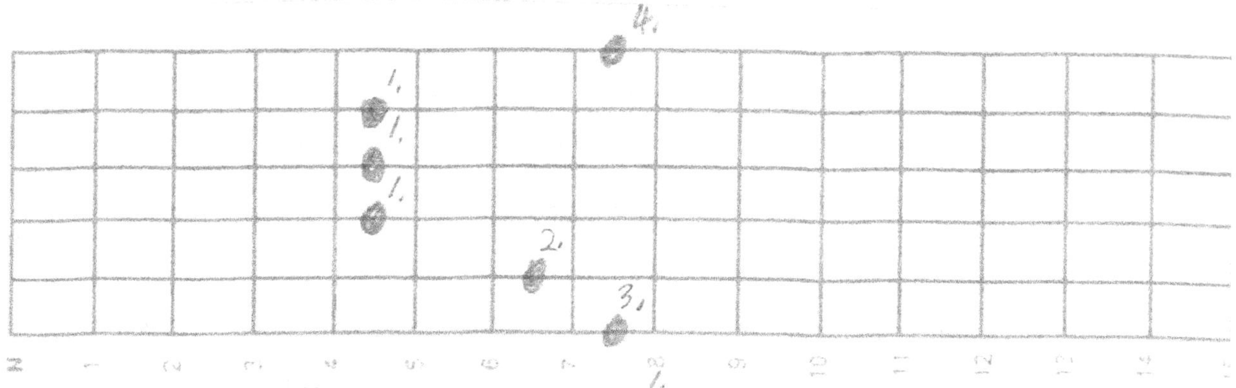

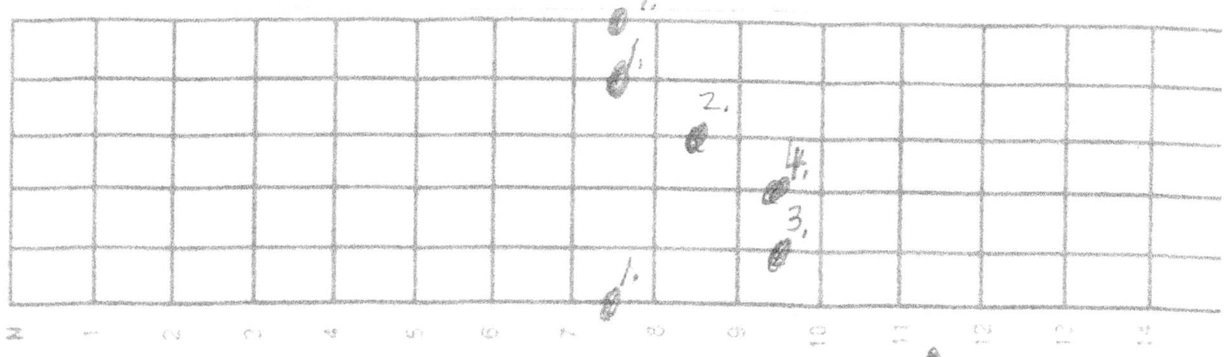

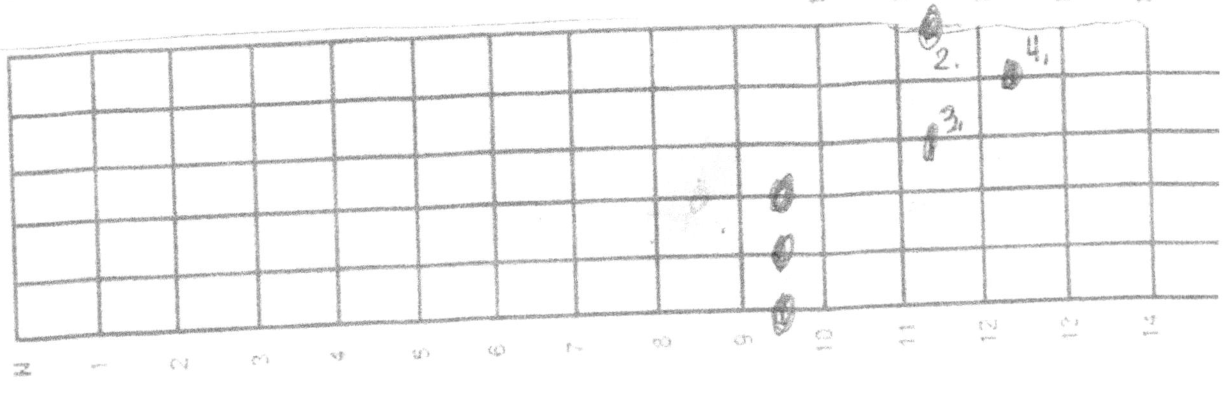

LEVEL 2
APPENDIX 2: Seven Short Flamenco Pieces:

3

No. 4 ALEGRIAS. I think at this point it is necessary to state that the basic rhythms of the ALEGRIAS, BULERIAS and the SOLEARES are the same, although there are of course differences in tempo and expression.

They are all basically in sections of **12** beats which could be written down either in four bars of **3/4** or **3/8**, or in one bar of **12/4**. In all cases the accents are practically unvarying. Here they are:–

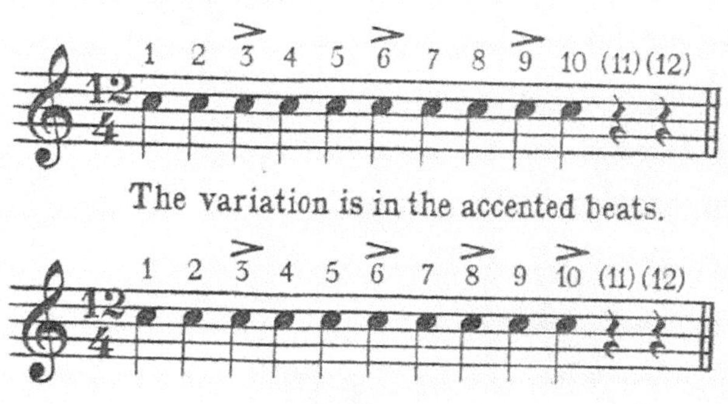

It could be felt in two sets of three and three sets of two with the last two beats tacet.

Although opinions differ over this, in my experience the 1 2 3, 1 2 3, 1 2, 1 2, is the most used.

Here is the same written in **3/4** (ALEGRIAS)

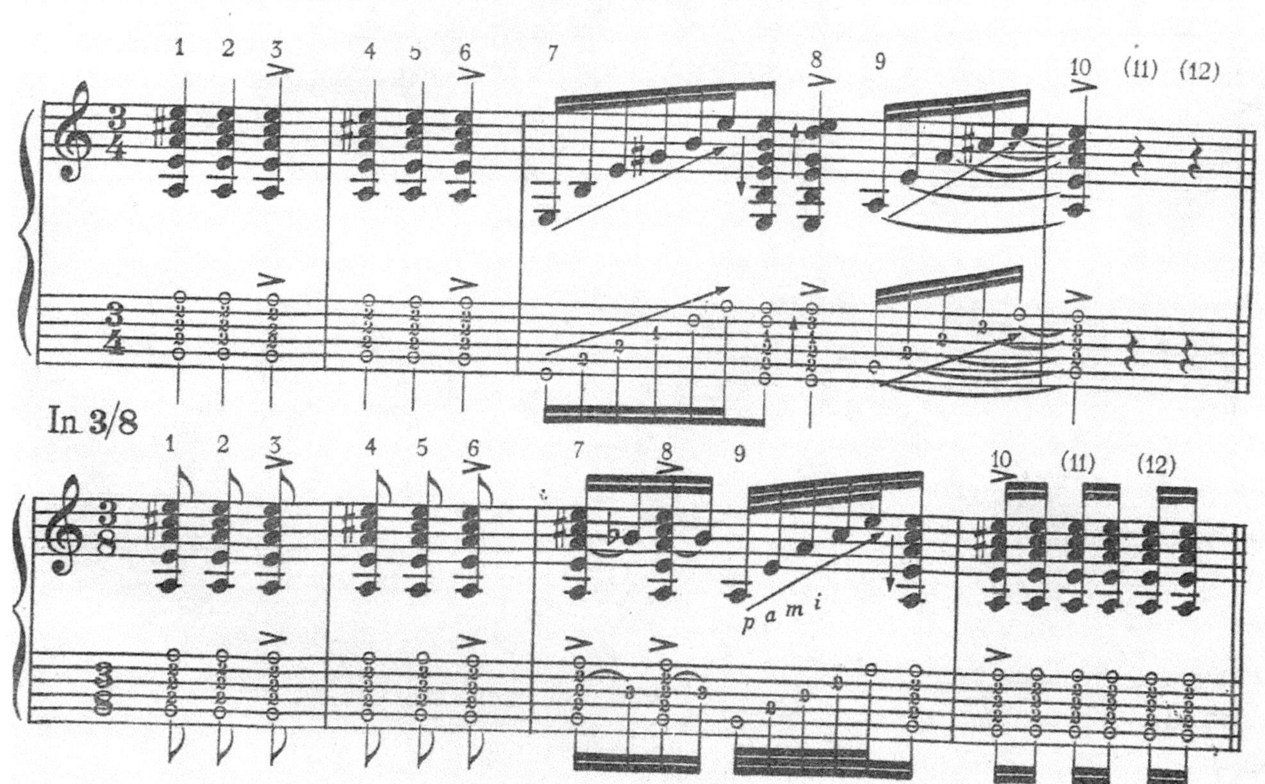

Alegrias

Cejilla at 7th Fret
♩. = 126
GUITAR
pami
CIFRA
HEEL
TAPS

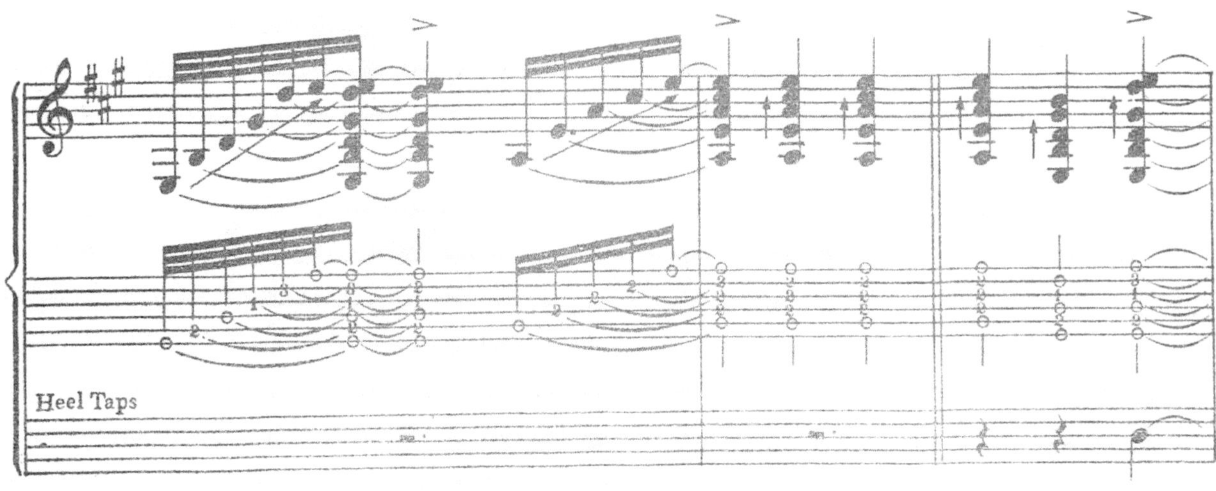
Heel Taps

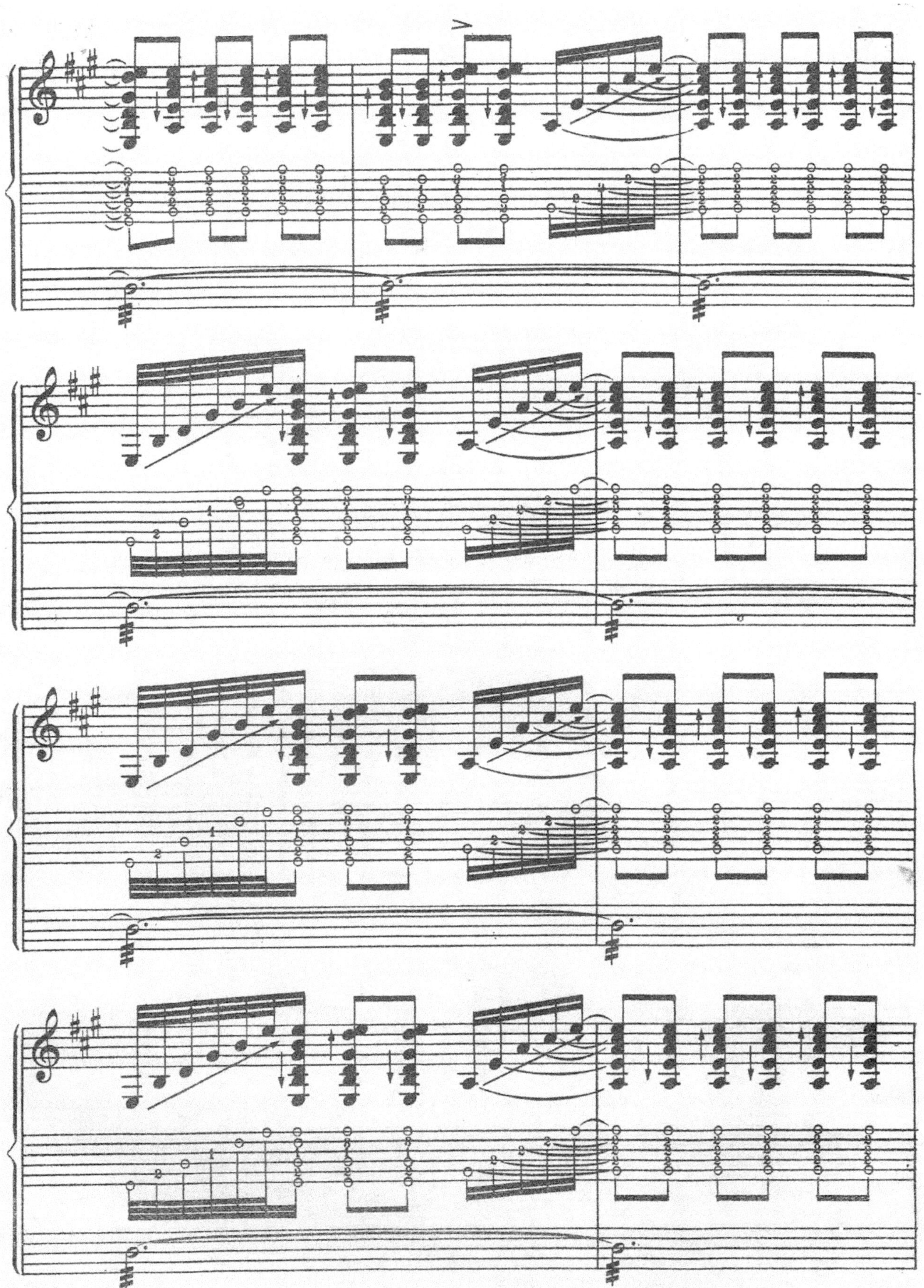

✲ Continous roll paqueno a.m.i.

HEELS

No. 2 is the Seguidillas and again an explanation of this rhythm is essential if it is to be understood. It is most easily understood if written in alternate bars of 3/4 and 6/8. There are accented and unaccented beats, and the main accented beats are as follows;—

The Seguidilla as you see commences on the second and third beats of the 3/4 bar in a sort of lead in to the first heavy beat of the 6/8. If you said the rhythm in words it would sound like this:—

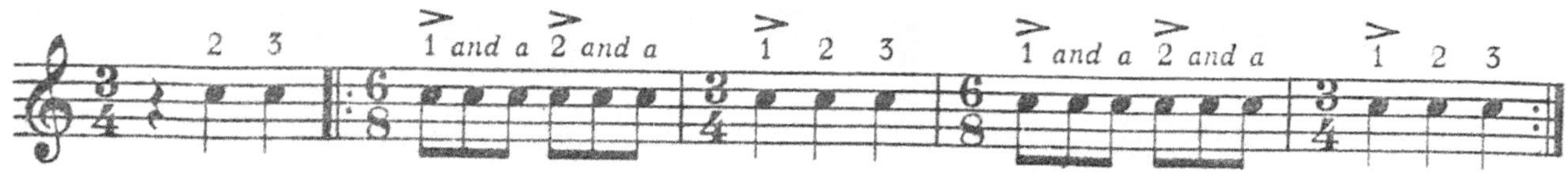

Note also very carefully that the SERRANAS is also in 3/4, 6/8 and is a Seguidilla in the key of E. The GUAJIRA is again in 3/4, 6/8 but a little faster than the SEGUIDILLA.

same as Seguidilla cuban but a little faster + both 6/8 + 3/4 + in Major key (A)

10. GUAJIRA

Cejilla at 7th Fret

p
p

p

2. SEGUIDILLAS

Cejilla at 7th Fret

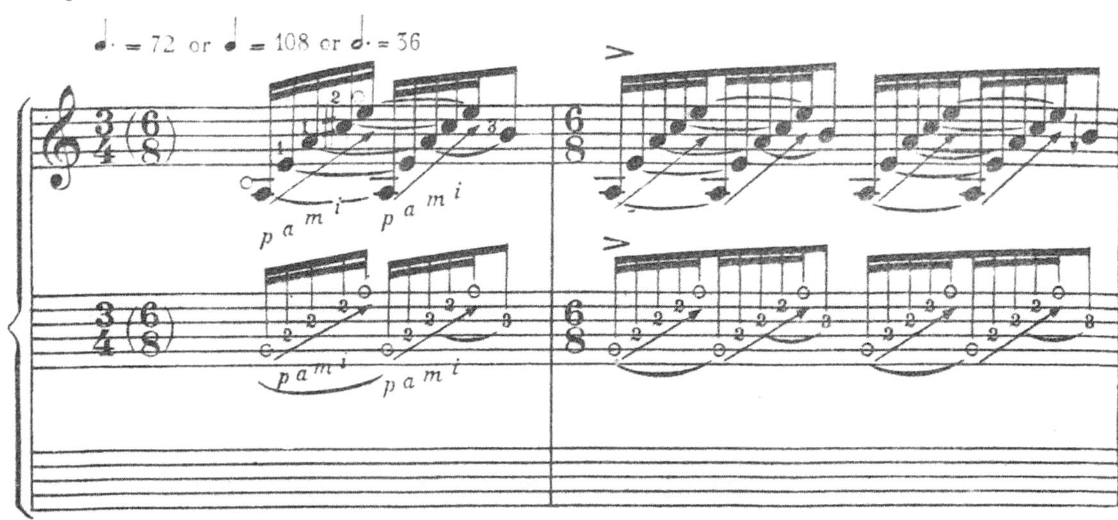

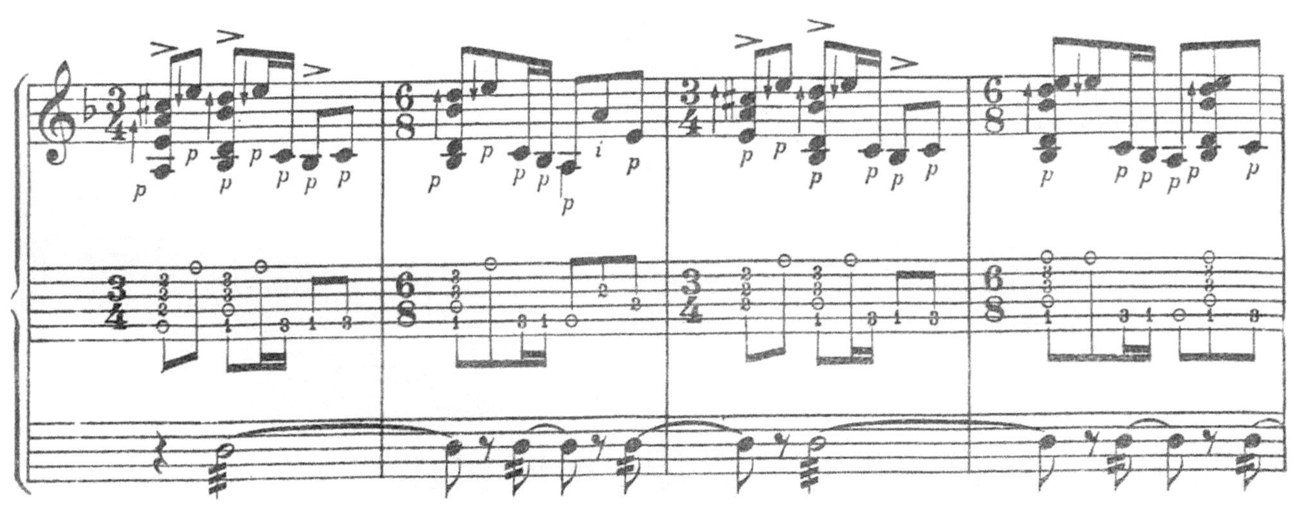

3. SEVILLANAS

Cejilla at 7th Fret

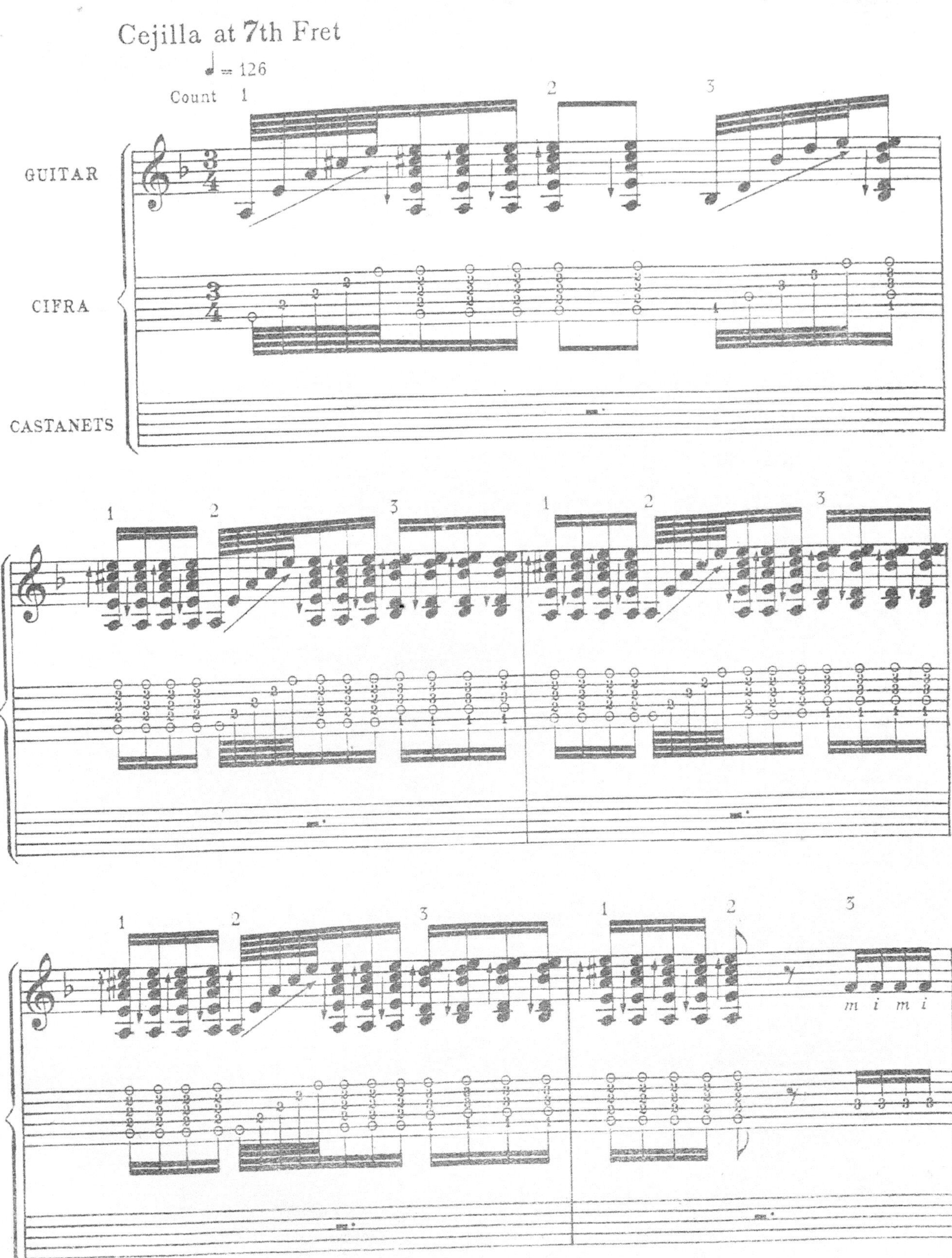

9. FARRUCA

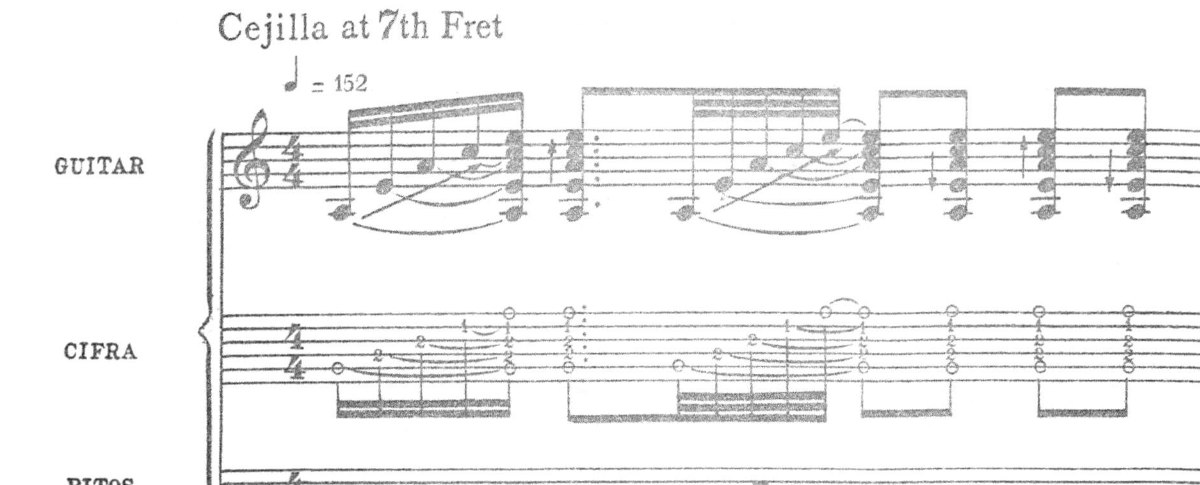

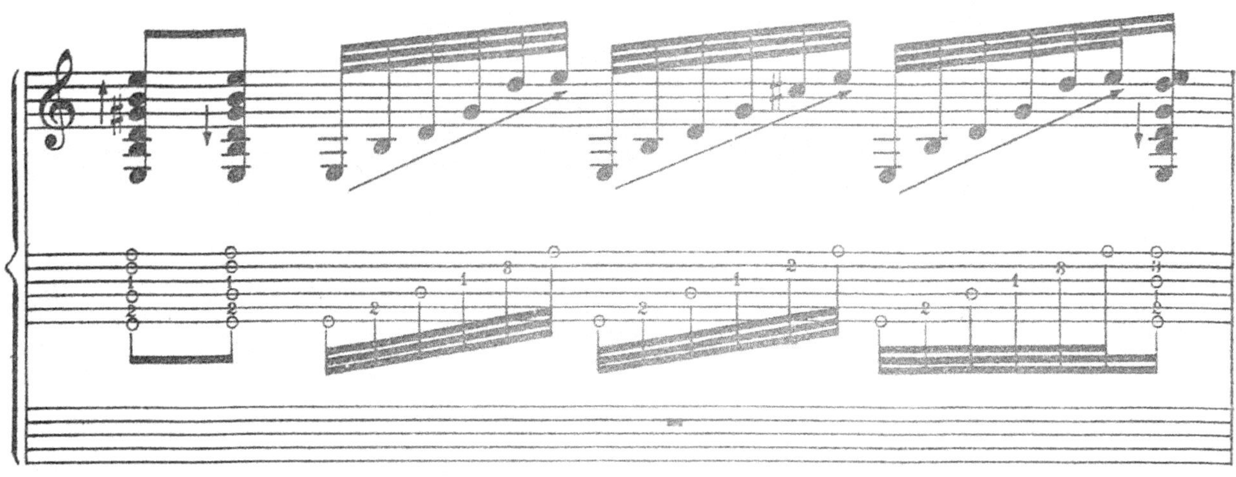

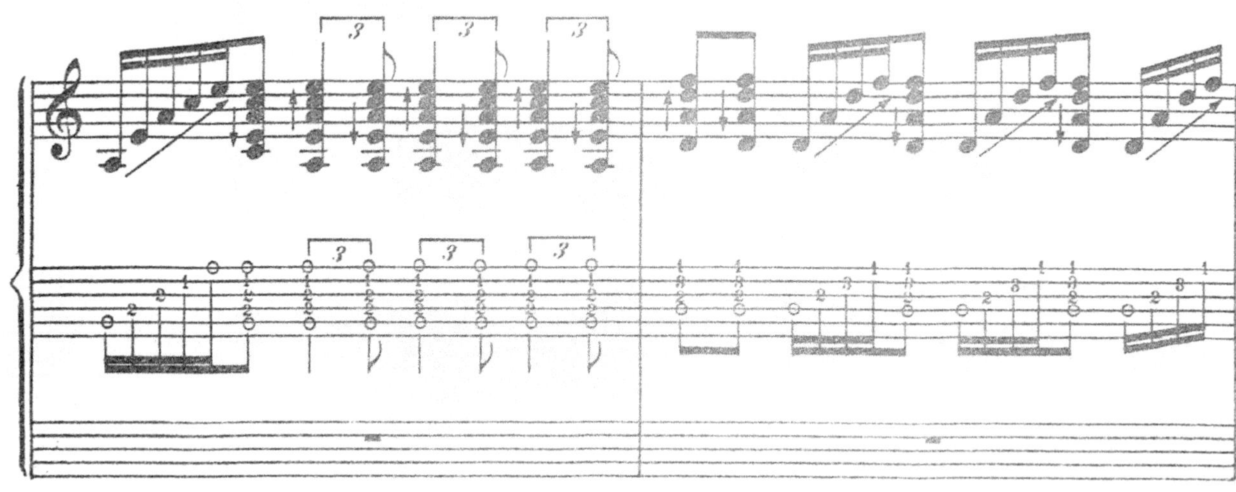

p
3
3

pami

LEVEL 3

APPENDIX 3: Indian Ragas

In putting together this section I wanted to include a couple complete raga's.
The graphics limitations of Amazon would not allow me to include them.
But if are interested you can send an email to: Acousticman1@hotmail.com. I will send a PDF with the missing 20 pages.10 pages each for the Ragas Todi and Chandranandan.

Quote Ali Akbar Khan (Sahib): “Music is health food for the soul, and the ears are the spoons with which we eat this food”

Quote: Ali Akbar Khan (Sahib): “Music is not for wealth or fame or even the pleasures of the mind, but is a path to genuine spiritual elevation. This I truly believe”.

Notation System is really quite simple.

Do Re Mi Fa Sol La Ti Do
Sa Re Ga Ma Pa Da Ni Sa

Usually written in three octaves each note is represented by a letter corresponding to the note of the scale. A dot above the “note” indicates the higher octave, a dot below the note indicates the lower octave. No dot above or below the note means it's in the middle (primary) octave. A LINE below the note indicates the note is flatted (one fret down).

Rainy Season Rag - Deshmalhar
Evening rag from Khammaj Tha

romantic

asc. arojati SRMP NS
desc. sampurnarojati RN DPDM GRG NS

R vadi P samvadi

RNDPDMGR GRS RNS also in desc.
Loneliness
Rag called Desh sans G, Deshmalhar w/ G

for girl waiting for lover
pathos love, romantic

jolly becomes sad
RMPDMGR RG SRNS

RGS RMPDMGR
RG must always return to S

classical NSRN DP light classical NSR NN DP

Chota Khayal (med fast) Satar Khani
(fast gat)

Barva tal

Khayal

Jhala Kirwani (Advanced class

S — — — | R — — — | G — — — | M — — — |

1) G G G G | G G G G | R R R R | R R S S | rep
dara da du ra du dara

2) | P P P P | M — — — | M M M M | G — — — |
G G G G | R — — — | R R R R | S — — — | rep

3) S S R R | G G M M | G — — — | R — — — |
R R G G | M M P P | D — — — | P — — — | rep

4) M D M D | P — — — | G P G P | M — — — |
R M R M | G — — — | S G S G | R — — — | rep

5) Ṡ — — — | N — — — | D D P P | M M P P |
M — — — | G — — — | R M G R | S — S — | rep

6) R — G — | M — — — | M — G — | R — — — |
G — M — | P — — — | P — M — | G — — — |
M — P | D — — — | P — M — | R — P — | rep

7) M — — | P — — — | D — — — | D — — — |
N — — | N — — — | D — — — | P — — — | rep

8) P — — — | D — — — | N — — — | N — — — | Ṗ — D — | M — — | N — D — | P — —

9) M | P | D | N | rep Ṡ | Ṡ | Ṡ | Ṡ | rep

10) Ṡ | Ṙ | Ġ | Ṙ | Ṡ | Ġ | Ṙ | Ṡ | Ṙ | Ṙ | N | D |
M | M | D | P | rep

Chan. 4

12) S S R R / R R G G / G G M M / M M P P

13) N Ṡ D N / P D M P / G M R G / S R N S /

Tihai S R G M / P D N Ṡ / S - S, Ṡ / - Ṡ
S Ṡ, Ṡ - Ṡ / S - - - / 2x
S R G M / P P D N Ṡ / S - S Ṡ / - Ṡ S - /
S Ṡ - S / Ṡ - - - /
S R G M / P D N Ṡ / S - S Ṡ / - Ṡ S - /
S S - S / Ṡ - - S / - S Ṡ - / - S - Ṡ /

Alap from Chandranandan

S N D S , S N D S

G S G M M P G S

R N D N S M G S

S S S N N S M G - S
ta na na ta na —— tawm

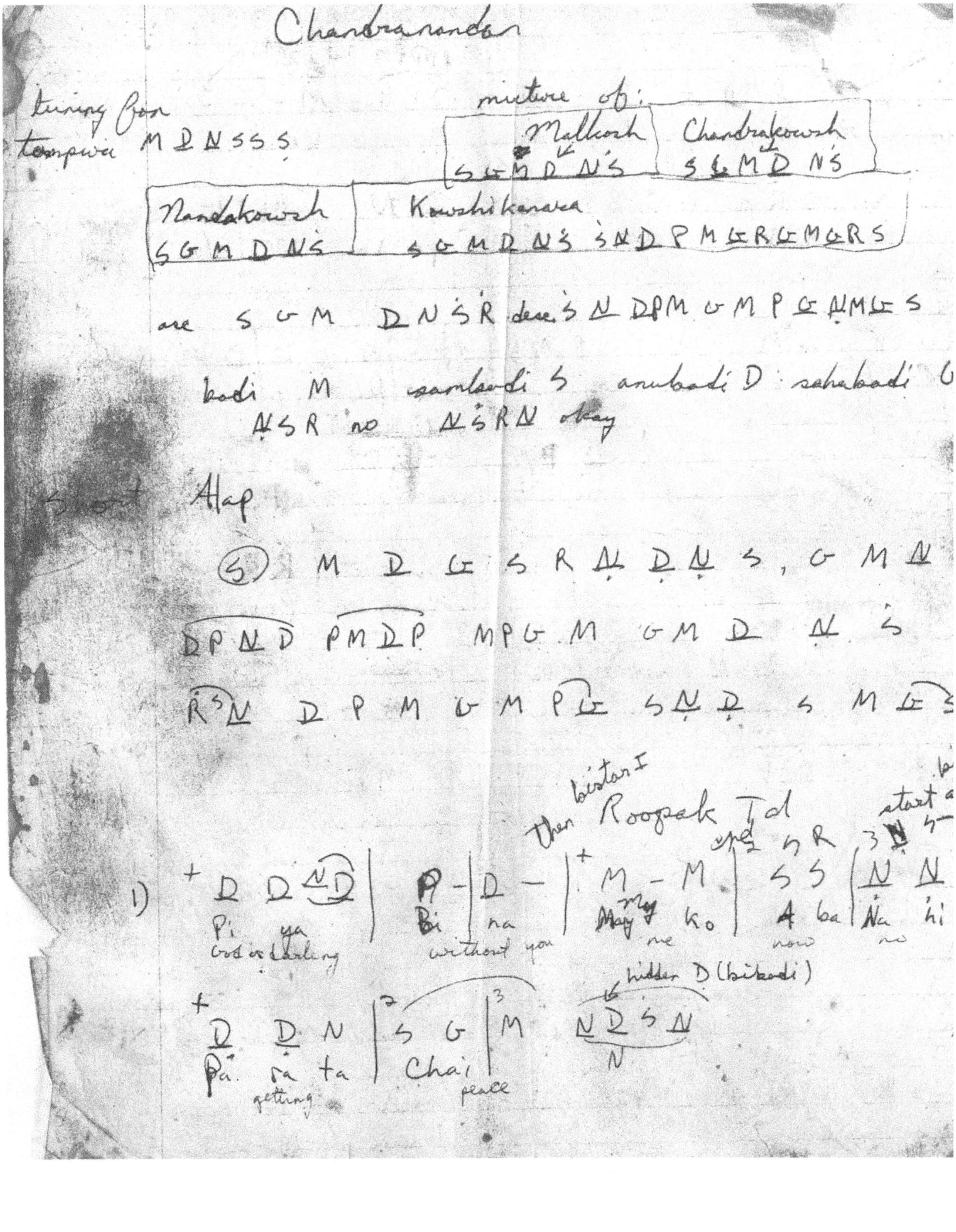

Chandranandan

tuning for tampura M D N S S S

mixture of:

Malkosh	Chandrakowsh
S G M D N Ṡ	S G M D N Ṡ

Nandakowsh	Kowshikanara
S G M D N Ṡ	S G M D N Ṡ Ṡ N D P M G R G M G R S

asc S G M D N Ṡ R desc Ṡ N D P M G M P G N M G S

badi M samvadi S anubadi D sahabadi G

N S R no N Ṡ R N okay

Short Alap

(S) M D G S R N D N S, G M N

D P N D P M D P M P G M G M D N Ṡ

Ṙ Ṡ N D P M G M P G S N D S M G S

Then bistar I Roopak Tal start a

1) + D D N D | P – | D – | + M – M | S S | N N

Pi ya | Bi | na | May ko | A ba | Na hi

God or darling | without you | me | now | no

+ D D N | S G | M N D S N

Pa ra ta | Chai

getting | peace

hidden D (bikodi)

LEVEL 4

Appendix Four: Here are the keys to fretboard freedom: (my personal Nirvana)

Mike "Jingles"/Paco de Lucia scale system CBAGFED

CBAGFED is the sequence of scale patterns up the neck. Play the C scale (pattern) in the open position, then the B scale (pattern) in the 1st position, then the A scale (pattern) in the 3rd position, the G scale (pattern) in the 5th position, then the F scale (pattern) in the 7th position, then the E scale (pattern) in the 9th position, then the D scale (pattern) in the 10th position. Doing all of this forms an overall pattern over the entire fretboard. You will have played all the notes in the key of C. Each scale pattern is a different mode of the key. No matter where you start in the sequence of CBAGFED the order of the scales never changes

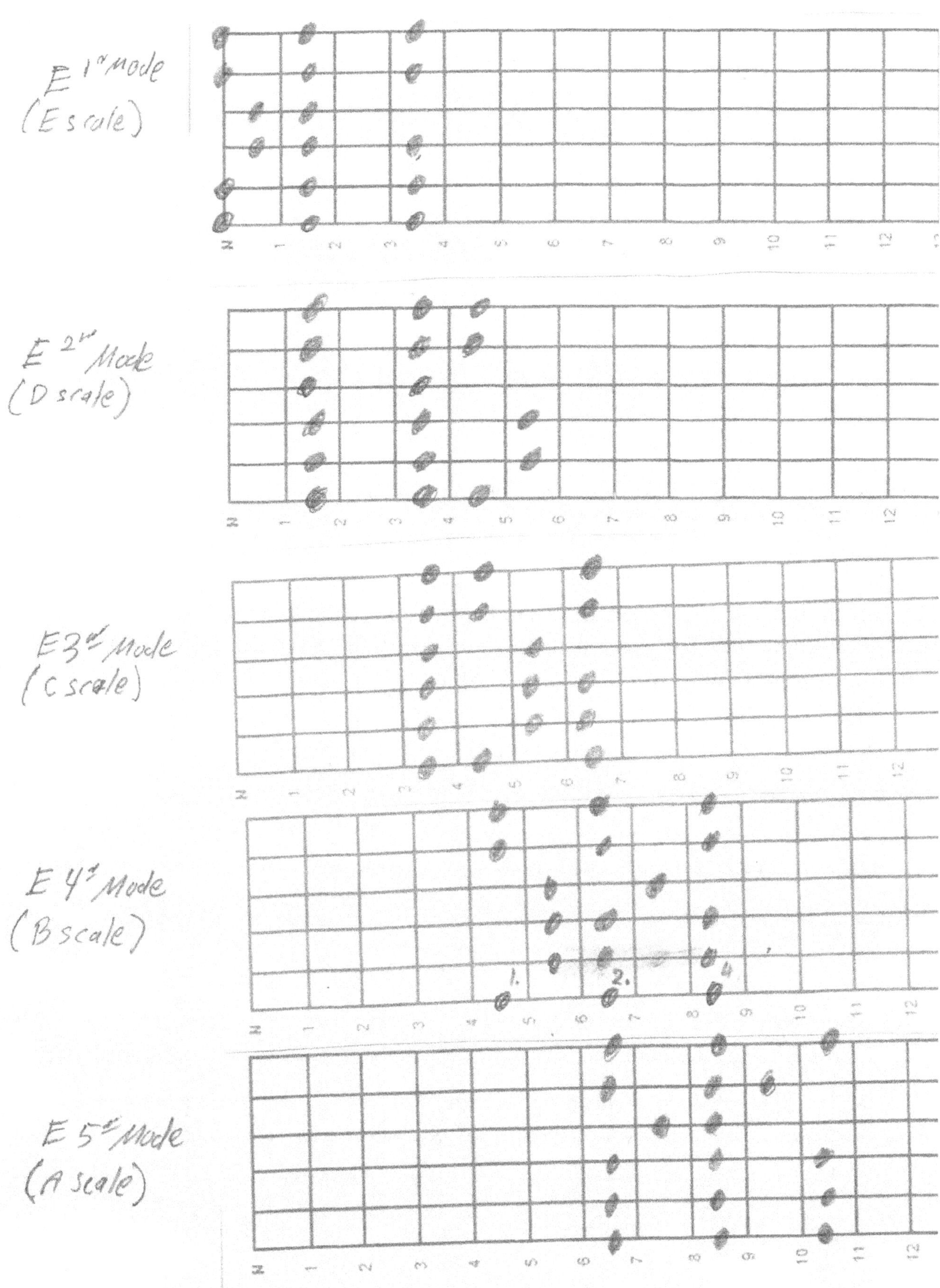
E 1st Mode
(E scale)
E 2nd Mode
(D scale)
E 3rd Mode
(C scale)
E 4th Mode
(B scale)
E 5th Mode
(A scale)
1.
2.
4

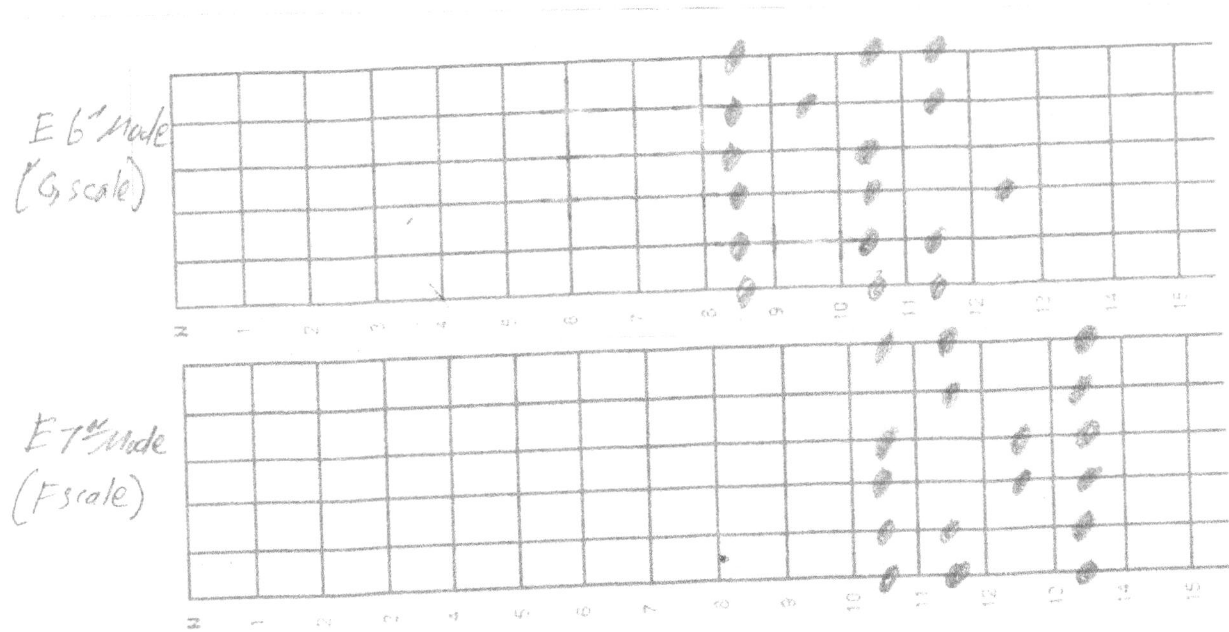

Here are all the notes in the key of C and B can you see the Pattern?   There is only one pattern for all keys and modes. The next page has AGFED. Learn it, Live it, Enjoy it! This the “Master Pattern” for the key of C Major.

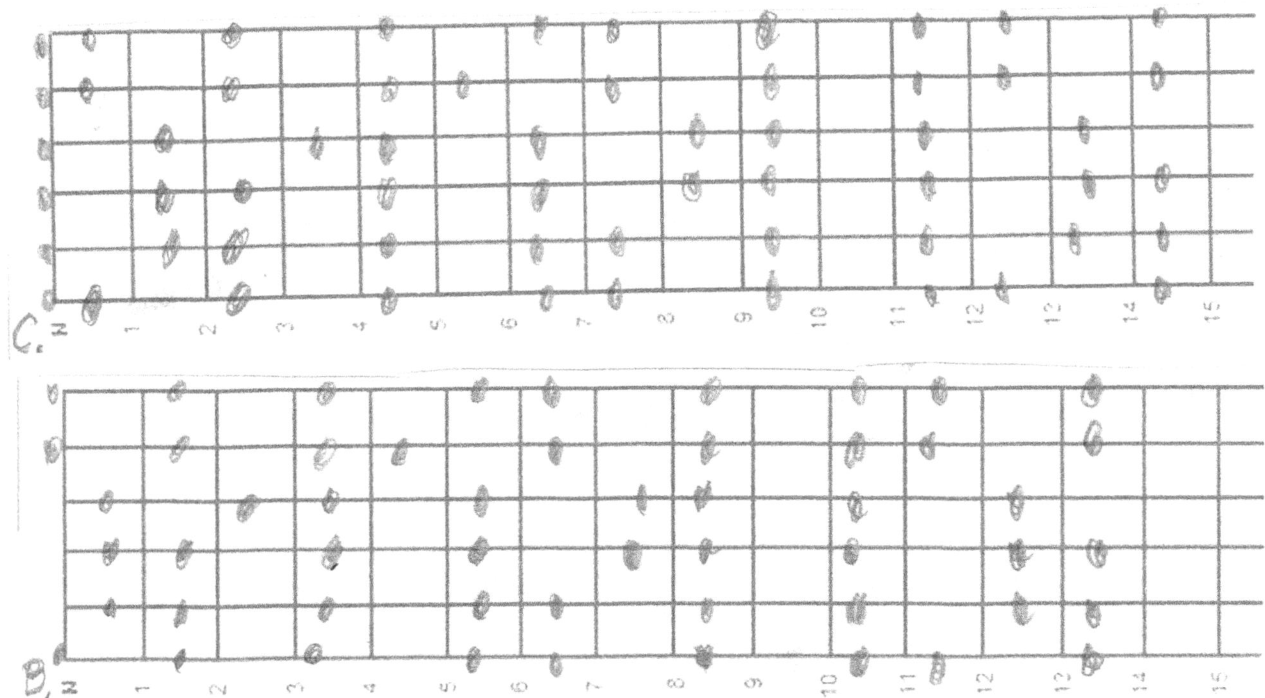

N 1 2 3 4 5 6 7 8 9 10 11 12 13 14

A.

N 1 2 3 4 5 6 7 8 9 10 11 12 13 14

G.

N 1 2 3 4 5 6 7 8 9 10 11 12 13 14

E

N 1 2 3 4 5 6 7 8 9 10 11 12 13 14

E.

N 1 2 3 4 5 6 7 8 9 10 11 12 13 14

D.

FREEDOM

If you practice every day playing the seven scale patterns that form each of the last seven overall fretboard patterns beginning with the first position in each key you will imprint the basic pattern on your brain. It's only seven scales, this is not rocket science. Take it in pieces, start with the key of E, then A, G, etc.

The overall pattern is always the same. If, for example you play and learn the seven mode patterns of the key of E, the overall fretboard pattern applies to all modes of all keys. The Master Pattern never changes, just the fret that you begin on. The final idea is to visualize the entire fretboard and the overlying Master Pattern. This way instead of looking at the fretboard and your brain telling your fingers what to play, (takes too long) the thought goes directly from your mentally visualized fretboard to your fingers. You will always know where every note is in every key. You will be completely free.

My teacher Mike Jingles said: "Now you know where all the notes are, what you play is up to you".

Good luck on your path , thanks for reading/listening!

Peter F. Walker
Woodstock, NY 2014
2014

www.ingramcontent.com/pod-product-compliance
Lightning Source LLC
LaVergne TN
LVHW061329060426
835513LV00015B/1339

* 9 7 8 1 9 3 9 3 7 4 0 3 5 *